Britain's Tree Story

The history and legends
of Britain's ancient trees

Britain's Tree Story

The history and legends of Britain's ancient trees

Julian Hight

National Trust

For my mother, the May Queen, who departed in the Autumn of her life.

We, gazing spellbound, feel our bodies swaying weak – as these ancient figures
Move and shimmer, and to our souls miraculously speak…

Pauline Ann Hight 5 May 1934 – 31 August 2010

First published in the United Kingdom in 2011 by
National Trust Books
10 Southcombe Street
London W14 0RA

An imprint of Anova Books Ltd

ISBN: 9781907892202

A CIP catalogue record for this book is available from the British Library.

18 17 16 15 14 13
10 9 8 7 6 5 4 3 2

Associate Publisher: Cathy Gosling

Designed and edited by SP Creative Design

Concept and cover design by Lee-May Lim

Repro by Dot Gradations Ltd, UK.

Printed by 1010 Printing International Ltd, China

This book can be ordered direct from the publisher at the website: www.anovabooks.com, or try your local bookshop. Also available at National Trust shops, including www.nationaltrustbooks.co.uk

Contents

Foreword

In human terms, ancient trees take a long time to develop – a couple of centuries for some species; a millennium or two for others, such as Oak and Yew. Even when they do eventually expire, they can still exist for many years as a standing dead or fallen tree and continue to evoke strong emotions. Too often, sadly, these trees and their legacy have been cleared away and lost, and although Britain has the largest number of ancient trees in northern Europe, we are still losing them at an alarming rate and much faster than they are being replaced.

This book documents some of the remarkable old trees that are known to have been lost in the past hundred years or so, many relatively recently. There is no doubt that countless others have also disappeared but have not been accounted for. The task of looking after the survivors is therefore vital, and, in doing this, we must try to take into account existing and future threats to their wellbeing.

The Ancient Tree Forum has been championing the values of old trees and their successors since its roots in the early 1990s. This book will contribute to public awareness of the significance, rarity and fragility of these trees, helping to conserve them and providing a record of trees that existed over 100 years ago as well as those surviving today. This ensures that many of the trees already lost, as well as ones that are clinging on, will be 'officially' recorded and will live on in photographs and stories, ensuring that the life of these historical and biological wonders can continue to be observed.

The National Trust cares for more ancient trees than any other organisation or individual and has many properties with significant concentrations of them. To become ancient, a tree must have plenty of space to grow and long continuity of benign management. This is why most ancient trees are found not in woods but in open areas and historic parks, both existing and lost. Trust parklands that have particular noted populations of very old trees are Calke Abbey, Derbyshire, Fountains Abbey, Yorkshire, Crom Estate, Fermanagh, Croft Castle, Herefordshire, and Dinefwr, Carmarthenshire. Formal avenues of ancient trees still line public roads, providing a wow factor for passing motorists, and there are particularly fine examples at Clumber Park, Nottinghamshire, and Kingston Lacy, Dorset.

Photographs and words add to our knowledge and appreciation of trees but are no substitutes for actually being in the presence of a truly ancient specimen and feeling overawed and inspired by it. This book could be the catalyst that encourages people to get out and find their own favourite old trees – fortunately, there are still many to be discovered and enjoyed!

Ray Hawes, National Trust

Introduction

Britain is one of the least forested countries in northern Europe but boasts the highest number of ancient trees. What we lack in woodland cover is almost made up for by the historical value of these sylvan beasts. Many have stood for over 1,000 years. One such tree, the Fortingall Yew in Scotland, is reputed to be up to four times that age, making it the oldest living organism in Europe.

From a human perspective, it is their constant presence within the community, surviving through one generation to the next and carrying events and stories, that elevates trees to a higher place in our psyche. Over the centuries, people have revered these sentinels and named them. They act as silent witnesses to our colourful history, and such is their longevity that some are only ten generations away from the end of the last ice age when they first colonised our islands, spreading north from the European mainland as the ice receded.

The inspiration for this book

I first thought of producing this book when I stumbled across an archive photograph of the Major Oak in Sherwood Forest whilst working for The Francis Frith Collection, a photographic archive of Britain dating back to 1860. I remembered visiting the tree as a child and dug out my own 'archive' photograph, which I had taken in 1976 (and, incidentally, I have included it in this book for posterity – my very first tree portrait). It soon became clear that one archive alone would not constitute a book if I were going to pay the subject any justice, so I set about acquiring photographs and prints from other sources.

Valentines, Judges, Photocrom and other local postcard publishers feature in this book with images dating from the period between 1880 and 1940. Most of the photographs were taken between 1903 and 1910 – the golden age of Victorian postcards. The fact that the manufacturers sold most of these cards as real photographic prints has given us a unique insight into the world as it was a century ago. The images provide a window to some of the oldest and largest trees ever recorded in Britain – in many cases, the only visual record of their existence.

Our great trees are also remembered in poems and texts by some of the greatest writers from history, so I have added these where possible to illustrate a wider picture, along with some beautiful engravings and paintings from the mid-nineteenth century.

It was an education and a pleasure to visit these trees where they still stand and to photograph them in the modern day for comparison. It led me on a journey from Perthshire to Cornwall and many places in between. Some of the trees have changed drastically, whereas others have hardly changed at all, lending credence to the idea of them being as old as tradition states or even considerably older. Each has its own distinct shape and character, which it carries with it throughout its lifetime. By visiting the places, I gleaned insightful local information that could not have been gained any other way, and for that I have the people of Britain to thank – their generosity and willingness to contribute confirmed my faith in the British public. Where I was unable to visit in person, invaluable help came from people in the field, and some of their photographs appear in this book for which I am very much indebted.

Trees and people

Many of the trees contained in this volume do not reside in forests but are found in heavily populated areas, on village greens, roadsides and other centres of human activity. Some have stood for millennia, a fact that confirms their place alongside humanity where they have struggled, excelled and survived amongst us. Trees and people have always worked together from the earliest times; mankind benefiting from timber, fruit and shade, and trees continuing to survive by replanting from their hosts although, admittedly, not always in equal measure. Huge swathes of forest were felled by neolithic peoples as they started to settle and farm the landscape – a practice that continues to this day – but working trees in the shape of ancient pollards are still visible in many of Britain's forests.

The demographic spread

Working on the directory, I realised how densely packed are the ancient trees around the Home Counties, with not too many in Wales, the far north of Scotland and Cornwall. There are good reasons for this. The climate in southeast England is kinder than other parts of Britain, making the trees' path through life easier and encouraging longevity, and many of the archive photographs focus on these areas, possibly because the sheer numbers of people living there dictated better sales for photographers. Many stories revolve around the deeds of monarchs, so the famed trees within these pages are often located near royal palaces and battlefields. They were protected under forest law, which accounts for why so many of them can still be seen today.

Trees in decline

Only half of the 60 Oaks featured still survive. An alarming number were burned down, usually by mischievous youths whose games ran out of control, the huge hollow trunks acting as chimneys to fuel the fire. Many more were felled by storms. The great storm of 1987 toppled 15 million trees at one fell swoop, highlighting the fact that Beech trees' shallow root systems do little to protect them; Oaks fared slightly better. However, although ancient trees were lost, proportionately they did quite well – their squat hollow trunks offering some defence to the elements.

Development is another factor in their decline, and the argument that 'they may become dangerous at some point in the future' is sometimes deemed sufficient reason to remove them. Others are so famous that they have literally disappeared at the hands of relic hunters keen to own a piece of history and destroying the subject in the process. The Elm fares rather worse. The British Elm population was decimated in the 1970s by Dutch Elm Disease, which, if handled more sympathetically (as in Brighton), could have been less devastating. Only two of the 15 Elms in this book survive – both in Brighton.

Sudden Oak Death (from America) has recently taken hold in southwest England and is spreading eastwards. It remains to be seen what impact this will have on the tree population, as English Oaks seem unaffected by it. Acute Oak Decline, which affects English Oaks, is more disquieting. It is worrying that so many ancient trees have disappeared in the last 30 years. Token replanting takes place and charities, such as the Woodland Trust and National Trust, are making great strides to reforest Britain.

Preserving our forests

Government plans to sell up to half of the woodlands run by the Forestry Commission were shelved under public pressure. A petition signed by 500,000 people demonstrated the British public's innate affinity with woodland. Ancient forests, such as Sherwood, The New Forest, Forest of Dean, Caledonian woods in Scotland and lesser-known but equally important sites, are the British equivalent of rain forest, locking up harmful CO2 gases, providing habitat for many species of wildlife and green spaces for the general public. Once gone, they are gone forever – it takes hundreds of years for these great trees to grow.

Organisations, such as the National Trust and Woodland Trust, play an important role in preserving woods and forests not owned by the state, and now could be a pivotal moment to ensure that no more are lost. By recognising that our ancient trees are as important as buildings and artefacts in the rich tapestry of British history, we can start protecting their survival.

The framework of this book

This book is set out in two parts: 'Natives' includes the trees that colonised Britain following the retreat of the last ice age 10,000 years ago; 'Invaders and Settlers' features the species introduced from foreign climes by invaders to our shores, travelling pilgrims or the tree hunters of the sixteenth to nineteenth centuries. I have divided each species by chapter and ordered them broadly as they appear on the map of Britain, working from north to south and east to west.

Finally, I make no apology for mixing history, myth and legend – they are, in my opinion, all equally valid in the life story of an ancient tree. Ancient trees are living links to our past, providing a fragile constant in an ever-changing world, and I hope they continue to play a role in our future. This is Britain's tree story, but it is also an island story, and a human one at that.

Directory of Trees

National Trust property   Tree still standing (2011)

The Oak

1   **The Birnam Oak**, Birnam, Perthshire
2   **Niel Gow's Oak**, Inver, Perthshire
3   **The Bruce Tree**, Strathleven, Dumbartonshire
4   **The Wallace Oak**, Elderslie, Renfrewshire
5   **The Druid's Oak**, Caton, Lancashire
6   **The Cowthorpe Oak**, Cowthorpe, Yorkshire
7   **The Shire Oak**, Headingley, Yorkshire
8   **The Allerton Oak**, Liverpool, Merseyside
9   **The Major Oak**, Edwinstowe, Nottinghamshire
10 **The Parliament Oak**, Edwinstowe, Nottinghamshire
11 **Robin Hood's Larder**, Edwinstowe, Nottinghamshire
12 **The Old Man of Calke**, Ticknall, Derbyshire
13 **The Bowthorpe Oak**, Manthorpe, Lincolnshire
14 **The Royal Oak**, Boscobel, Staffordshire
15 **The Shelton Oak**, Shrewsbury, Shropshire
16 **The Midland Oak**, Leamington Spa, Warwickshire
17 **The Battle Oak**, Mortimer's Cross, Herefordshire
18 **The Holgate Oak**, Kingsland, Herefordshire
19 **The Queen's Oak**, Potters Pury, Northamptonshire
20 **The Gospel Oak**, Polstead, Suffolk
21 **The Old Oak**, Ross-on-Wye, Herefordshire
22 **The Lassington Oak**, Gloucester, Gloucestershire
23 **The Newland Oak**, Newland, Gloucestershire
24 **Merlin's Oak**, Carmarthen, Carmarthenshire
25 **Elizabeth's Oak**, Hatfield Park, Hertfordshire
26 **The Minchenden Oak**, Southgate, London
27 **The Pulpit Oak**, Epping Forest, Essex
28 **Harold's Oak**, Epping Forest, Essex
29 **The Fairlop Oak**, Fairlop, Essex
30 **Turpin's Oak**, East Finchley, London
31 **The Elfin Oak**, Kensington Gardens, London
32 **Martin's Oak**, Richmond Park, London
33 **Herne's Oak**, Windsor Great Park, Berkshire
34 **The Conqueror's Oak**, Windsor Great Park, Berkshire
35 **Offa's Oak**, Windsor Forest, Berkshire
36 **The Victoria Oak**, Windsor Forest, Berkshire
37 **The Wilberforce Oak**, Keston, Kent
38 **The Oldest Oak**, Knole Park, Kent
39 **The Seven Oaks**, Sevenoaks, Kent
40 **The Lingfield Oak**, Lingfield, Kent
41 **The Sidney Oak**, Penshurst, Kent
42 **St Dunstan's Oak**, Headcorn, Kent
43 **The Old Oak Tree Restaurant**, Cobham, Surrey
44 **The Crouch Oak**, Addlestone, Surrey
45 **The Leith Hill Oak**, Dorking, Surrey
46 **The King's Oak**, Tilford, Surrey
47 **Queen Elizabeth's Oak**, Cowdray Park, Sussex
48 **Queen Elizabeth's Oak**, Northiam, Sussex
49 **The Knightwood Oak**, New Forest, Hampshire
50 **The King and Queen Oaks**, New Forest, Hampshire
51 **The Eagle Oak**, New Forest, Hampshire
52 **The Big Belly Oak**, Savernake Forest, Wiltshire
53 **The King Oak**, Savernake Forest, Wiltshire
54 **The Braydon Oak**, Savernake Forest, Wiltshire
55 **Gog and Magog**, Glastonbury, Somerset
56 **Cromwell's Oak**, Melksham, Wiltshire
57 **The Turkey Oaks**, Wiltshire
58 **Wyndham's Oak**, Silton, Dorset
59 **The Meavy Oak**, Meavy, Devon
60 **The Last Oak in England**, Penzance, Cornwall

The Elm

The Beech

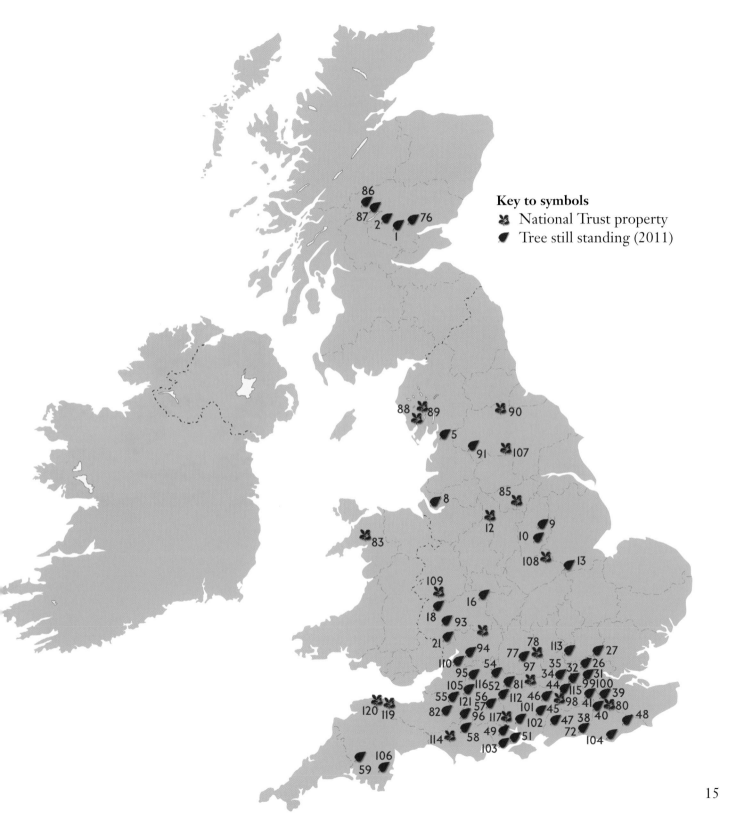

Key to symbols

🌼 National Trust property

🌰 Tree still standing (2011)

Estimating the Age of a Tree

Apart from knowing the planting date, the only way to accurately record the age of a tree is to count the annual growth rings within its trunk. Obviously, one cannot cut down a healthy tree to count the rings, but, using an auger, a core sample can be removed from the tree and analysed for accurate counting. However, even this method is still far from ideal – why vandalise an ancient tree just to satisfy a curiosity? A further problem faced when using an auger is that the heartwood from ancient trees frequently rots away, leaving a chasm that is impossible to date. Only the outer rings or 'sapwood' provide nourishment to the tree, and hence it can survive quite happily with a completely hollow trunk. In fact, to some degree this can provide storm protection – a cylindrical object offering more resistance to bending than a solid one, a principle used to good effect by John Smeaton with his lighthouse design based on the properties of an Oak tree. However, for most purposes, a general figure will suffice and, by using the data from known ancient trees, it is possible to place most within approximate age brackets.

Generally, the longer-living species grow more slowly than the shorter-lived ones. Thus a Yew, our longest-lived tree, can take 500 years to reach a girth of 4m (13.1ft) while an English Oak may take around 200 years, and a Hawthorn would be lucky ever to reach that size at all.

Trees generally live through three stages of life – youth, maturity and decline – so different species are termed ancient depending on which stage they have reached. A tree with a reducing crown and gnarled, heavy, hollow trunk is likely to be older than a larger crowned mature one. Factors such as climate and location can also have an effect. A tree occupying a sheltered position in a temperate climate will produce wider annual rings and therefore have a larger girth than one in a cold, exposed position – for instance, in a southern English hollow as opposed to an exposed northern crag. Individual trees in the same location can also grow at different rates, much like people, who all grow into different shapes and sizes.

The trees mentioned here are measured around the girth of the trunk at 1.5m (4.92ft) from the ground (with the exception of Yews, which are generally measured near the ground), but it is not always possible to do this, especially if there are large growths and bumps that can make the measurement inaccurate. In this case, moving to the narrowest point of the trunk – the waist of the tree – gives a reasonable estimate.

A rough guide to estimating the age of Yews and Oaks can be found opposite, but do remember that there are exceptions to every rule, and the individual growing conditions and life events of each tree will cause it to grow at a different rate.

Age estimator: Yew

Girth of tree	Age in years
1m	100
3m	300
4m	500
6m	800
10m	2,000

Age estimator: Oak

Girth of tree	Age in years
2m	80
4m	200
6m	400
8m	800
10m	1,000

Size conversion chart

Metric	Imperial
1m	3ft 3in
3m	9ft 8in
4m	13ft 1in
6m	19ft 7in
10m	32ft 8in

RIGHT: The weathered trunk of an ancient oak – host to a myriad of life forms.

NATIVES

This section focuses on trees that are native to Britain –
these are the trees that colonised the British Isles following
the retreat of the last ice age, around 10,000 years ago.

CHAPTER ONE

The Oak

Pendunculate Oak (*Quercus robur*);
Sessile Oak (*Quercus petrea*)

ABOVE: Oak flower.
OPPOSITE: A lone Oak in the New Forest, Hampshire.

As Britain's largest native tree, the Oak has come to symbolise the very essence of England. As the lion is king of the jungle, so the Oak is king of the forest. The most renowned of all our trees in fable and history, it is our most important woodland tree, providing a habitat for more wildlife species than any other. It can grow to a height of 45m (147.6ft) and attain a remarkable girth up to 14m (45.93ft) according to the waist-measurement of the giant Cowthorpe Oak in Yorkshire, now long gone, which could reputedly hold 40 men. On one memorable occasion, 70 people, including children perched on shoulders, crammed inside its cavernous bole.

Oak has long been valued for house- and ship-building due to its great strength as well as its boughs, which allow natural 'knees' to be cut at various angles, but much of the oak forests that covered the country are now gone. However, plenty of fine trees can still be found. An Oak can live for 20 years before bearing fruit – the familiar acorn, which provides food for birds and squirrels and, in days gone by, for 'pannage', which was a common right for fattening swine on acorns and is still observed in the New Forest. Although poisonous to ponies, acorns were ground into meal to make bread in times of hardship.

The direct translation of the Latin name reads *Quercus* (oak) and *robur* (strength), alluding to the physical and spiritual power that the mighty Oak tree has long held over us.

The Birnam Oak

BIRNAM, PERTHSHIRE |

Nestled in a strip of woodland on the sandy south bank of the River Tay, the Birnam Oak is famous for being the sole survivor of ancient Birnam Wood. In Macbeth, Shakespeare names it as the oaken forest where Malcolm and his soldiers cut branches and held them aloft for camouflage as they marched toward Dunsinane Hill 15 miles away – Macbeth's stronghold – and fulfilled the three witches' prophecy:

> *Macbeth shall never vanquish'd be until*
> *Great Birnam wood to high Dunsinane hill*
> *Shall come against him.*

From *Macbeth*, William Shakespeare

The rest, as they say, is history, with Macbeth meeting his bloody end.

With a hollow gnarled trunk measuring 7m (22.9ft) in girth, the tree certainly appears worthy of inspiring the Bard's immortal lines. It may not have been standing at the time of Macbeth's death in 1057 but, at around 600 years old the tree is seen as the last survivor of the Great Birnam Wood. It sits in the heart of Perthshire's 'Big Tree Country' and is flanked by a 300-year-old Sycamore, which, although larger in size, is probably only half the age of the old Oak.

Let every soldier hew him down a bough
And bear't before him: thereby shall
*   we shadow*
The numbers of our host and make
*   discovery*
Err in report of us.

Bring it after me.
I will not be afraid of death and bane
Till Birnam Forest come to Dunsinane.

As I did stand my watch upon the hill,
I look'd toward Birnam, and anon,
*   methought,*
The wood began to move.

From *Macbeth*, William Shakespeare

ABOVE: The Birnam Oak in 2009.
LEFT: The Birnam Oak, c. 1925.

Niel Gow's Oak

Just a mile-and-a-half upstream along the River Tay from Birnam stands a large Oak named after Niel Gow (1727–1807), Perthshire's most renowned fiddler. He lived and died in Inver village and often composed and played beneath the shade of this great tree. He was famous for writing some of Scotland's favourite strathspeys, many of which are still heard today at Scottish dances.

The tree has a girth of 6m (19.68ft), and carved into an oak bench beneath it are the fitting words of the contemporary Scottish singer/songwriter Michael Marra:

Sit beneath the fiddle tree,
with the ghost of Niel Gow next to me.

I sat beneath the tree, but not having my guitar to hand, I sang these lines instead, barely audible above the din of the roaring A9 road, a problem that Niel Gow would not have had to contend with.

ABOVE: Niel Gow by Sir Henry Raeburn, *c.* 1793.
BELOW: Neil Gow's Oak in 2009.

The Bruce Tree
STRATHLEVEN, DUMBARTONSHIRE 3

This fine tree stood 8.8m (28.87ft) in girth and 5.5m (18ft) high and, at between 700 and 1,000 years old, it was one of the oldest Oaks in Scotland before it fell in May 2004 after a fire was set within its hollow trunk.

The Strathleven Artizans, a voluntary group promoting historical links with Robert the Bruce, discovered that Bruce himself had owned the surrounding estate when the tree was a mere youngster, and henceforth the Oak became known locally as 'The Bruce Tree'. Whilst cutting up the tree, the Artizans were surprised to see the image of a face appear within the heart of the great Oak. This cemented their view that it was indeed the Bruce Tree, symbolically displaying a likeness of the heroic Scottish king. An ancient acorn was also found there in a small hole, which over the centuries had itself petrified into wood.

As his final wish, Bruce asked his champion Sir James Douglas to carry his heart to the Church of The Holy Sepulchre in Jerusalem in redemption for his unfulfilled vow of leading a crusade to the Holy Land. However, Sir James fell fighting against the Moors in Spain and never completed the task. The Strathleven Artizans have carved a wooden heart from the Bruce Tree and they plan to fulfil Bruce's final wish by taking it to Israel themselves.

Hard by the water side,
A giant oak uprears its head,
And seems to guard the river's bed.
Spreading its stalwart arms around,
Till here and there they sweep the ground.

From *Robert The Bruce*, Alexander W M Clark Kennedy, 1884

Planted for War, Carved for Love
The Strathleven Artizans

ABOVE: Is this the face of Robert the Bruce?

LEFT: The Bruce Tree shortly after it fell in June 2004.

The Wallace Oak
ELDERSLIE, RENFREWSHIRE 4

William Wallace was a thirteenth-century knight who was famous for leading the resistance against the English during the Wars of Scottish Independence. Legend holds that Wallace, along with 300 of his men, took refuge in the branches of an Oak on his father's estate in Elderslie, where he was born in 1272, to avoid an English patrol. He continually avoided pursuit until 23 August 1305 when he was betrayed and turned over to English troops by a Scottish knight who was loyal to Edward I. Wallace was tried for treason in London, crowned with a garland of oak leaves and dragged naked at the heels of a horse to Smithfield for execution where he was hung, drawn and quartered. His severed head was preserved in tar and was displayed for all to see on London Bridge.

The Wallace Oak eventually fell during a great storm in 1856 but not before J G Strutt had made a fine drawing of it for his *Sylva Britannica*.

The tree was described before its demise as 'a melancholy torso, bald and frail, with its limbs hacked off by relic hunters, like Wallace's by the hangman'. Whether the tree was large enough to have held so many men is questionable, but it was calculated that its branches covered 413 square metres (495 square yards), making it an immense size.

Today the tree reputedly survives in the form of two regency tables, which were sold at auction in 2001. Whether this is true or not, the memory of Scotland's revered national hero William Wallace undoubtedly lives on.

BELOW: *The Wallace Tree*, drawn by A Nasmyth, engraved by W Miller, c.1830.

The Druid's Oak

CATON, LANCASHIRE 5

Set in the Lower Lune valley, the Druid's Oak has stood for centuries at Caton. At the foot of the tree are some small stone steps, known as the Fish Stones. These once acted as a marketplace where the medieval monks from nearby Cockersands Abbey sold the salmon they had fished from the River Lune, which flows over the old tree's roots.

The Oak still stands, but after concerns from the local villagers about its declining condition, a new tree was grown from one of its acorns. It was planted within the shell of the hollow 4-m (13-ft) trunk on 22 April 2007 by the High Sheriff of Lancashire.

The irony is that, as it grows, the new tree will inevitably destroy its parent, making the rare preservation order placed on the tree next to worthless.

ABOVE: The Druid's Oak in 2007.
BELOW: The Druid's Oak in 1905.

The Druids

The Druids were the priesthood for the Celtic tribes of pre-Christian Britain, and they could be men or women. Being mostly disparate and warlike, the tribes were unified by this intellectual class, who acted as judges and oversaw the community's education, medicine, history and science, basing their religion on astrology and astronomy and using trees as sacred symbolism.

Their tradition was mainly oral, the earliest writings about them appearing in the second century BC from Greek and Roman sources. Julius Caesar is quoted as saying that they were deliberately non-literate so as not to encourage students to 'neglect the cultivation of the memory'. This literary silence enabled them to maintain a secrecy and mystery around their knowledge, no doubt enhancing the power they held over their community. Apprentice Druids would memorise the teachings by oral instruction for up to 20 years before being admitted fully into the order. However, when needed, it is thought that they may have used a system of writing known as Tree Ogham, or Tree Alphabet, to keep records and make inscriptions. Called Beth-Luis-Nion after its first letters, much as our common ABC, each letter was named after and connected to a sacred tree. It remains inscribed on over 400 standing stones in Ireland and Britain but it is believed to have been written also on Birch bark, none of which survives to this day, of course.

The Druids held the Oak in the highest esteem and used Oak trees to form he groves where they performed their religious rites. Anything that grew in them was deemed sacred, including the mistletoe that they also revered:

The sacred oaks
Among whose awful shades the Druids strayed,
To cut the hallow'd mistletoe, and hold High converse
with their gods.
Pliny the Elder (died AD79)

In AD61, Suetonius, the Roman governor of Britain, sent his legions to destroy the remaining Druids, who by this time had gathered at their stronghold, the Isle of Anglesey. The Romans did this in no uncertain terms by massacring the entire Druid population, and, for good measure, they also burnt down their sacred Oak groves. When describing the Druids, Julius Caesar wrote:

Some of them make use of giant wickerwork images, the limbs of which are packed with living men; they are set alight, and the men perish in the inferno.

The Druids are reputed to have taken their name from the Greek word for the tree, *drys*, and the Proto-Indo-European word, *wied*, meaning to see. Hence Druid means 'oak knowledge'.

LEFT: Mistletoe.

The Cowthorpe Oak
COWTHORPE, YORKSHIRE 6

Compared with this, all other trees are children of the Forest.
From *Evelyn's Sylva*, Dr Hunter, 1786

Three miles from Wetherby, the Yorkshire village of Cowthorpe was the birthplace of this majestic tree, which holds the record for being the largest girthed English Oak ever in Britain. In 1804, it had a girth of 14.32m (46.9ft) at 1.8m (5.9ft) from the ground. Its hollow trunk was said to have once held 70 people, with the children sitting on adult shoulders.

Oliver Cromwell used the neighbouring village of Tockwith as a staging post before the Battle of Marston Moor in 1644, and the tree would have been a major landmark in his time. One hundred and fifty years ago, a Dr Hunter claimed that the tree was 1,600 years old. Legend names Cowthorpe as the birthplace of Guido Fawkes, infamous for his part in the failed 1605 Gunpowder Plot.

According to *Langdale's Topographical Dictionary of Yorkshire*, in 1822 its principal limb extended 14.6m (48ft) from the trunk. Its leading branch had fallen in 1718 – its crash alarming the neighbourhood residents – and was found to weigh over five tons.

The tree is believed to have died in the 1950s. Although heavily propped in the photograph opposite, it still looked in great shape with plenty of strong branches and a good crop of leaves, although it had clearly lost its top, giving it a short, squat appearance.

Now all that remains is a rotting stump, but an acorn from the Cowthorpe Oak was planted at Runciman Farm in Drury, New Zealand, in the 1870s. Known as the Runciman Oak, the tree now has a girth of almost 5m (16.4ft) at 0.5m (1.6ft) from the ground and is starting to show the characteristics of an ancient tree – its growth perhaps accelerated by the temperate climate. In turn, the tree has been used to propagate a whole avenue of young Oaks, ensuring that the descendants of the Cowthorpe Oak survive on the other side of the world.

*An oak whose boughs were mossed
with age,
and high top bald with dry antiquity.*
William Shakespeare describing the Cowthorpe Oak in *As You Like It*, c.1600

OPPOSITE: The Cowthorpe Oak, c. 1903.

BELOW: The Cowthorpe Oak from *The Illustrated London News*, 1857.

The Shire Oak

HEADINGLEY, YORKSHIRE 7

The Shire Oak was already an ancient tree when Jacob Strutt made an engraving *c.*1700, and must have been of substantial size in Saxon times when it is believed to have become the meeting place of the Skyrack Wapentake. A 'wapentake' was a territorial area or government district, and the term 'skyrack' may have derived from 'shire oak' as it was customary for a wapentake to be named after its meeting place. The men of the wapentake would assemble there to settle legal disputes and make important local decisions. It was also the rallying point for an army in times of war.

On 26 May 1941, the ancient stump collapsed during a furious gale and was later removed. However, a section was saved and this was carved into a likeness of the Madonna and Child. It can now be seen in the Lady Chapel of nearby St Michael's Church.

The tree gave its name to the two pubs opposite the church, namely The Skyrack and The Original Oak. The latter has mounted a commemorative plaque on the outside of its garden wall.

All his leaves,
Fall'n at length,
Look, he stands,
Trunk and bough,
Naked strength.

From *The Foresters*, Alfred, Lord Tennyson, *c.*1891

ABOVE: The Shire Oak, *c.*1910.

LEFT: The Shire Oak in 1903.

The Allerton Oak

CALDERSTONES PARK, LIVERPOOL, MERSEYSIDE 8

The Allerton Oak, which stands in Calderstones Park, has a girth of 5.5m (18ft) and has been there for up to 1,000 years. The park itself takes its name from the remains of a Bronze Age cairn, which was dismantled in the early nineteenth century. The six sarcen monoliths that were used in the construction of the burial chamber now sit in a glass house in the park.

The Allerton 'hundred' or wapentake (local council) met beneath the tree's branches for court sittings in medieval times, so the area and, in particular, the Oak, must have held significant local importance.

In 1864, a gunpowder ship, the *Lotty Sleigh*, which was moored in Garston docks on the River Mersey, caught fire and exploded whilst carrying 10 tons of gunpowder. The actual blast triggered a mini-earthquake, which carried three miles to Calderstones Park and split the Allerton Oak in two. Almost 150 years later, we find the tree in remarkably good health.

Around the year 1907, some metal posts were erected in order to support the tree's ageing branches and they remain in place today.

Every autumn, the Oak yields up to 100,000 acorns, and the gene pool remains safe, thanks to local councillors, who were so concerned for the tree's welfare during the Second World War that they grew saplings and gave them to troops to plant all over the world, wherever they were stationed.

ABOVE: The hollow split trunk refuses to give in, 2009.

LEFT: A picture postcard of the Allerton Oak in 1907.

By the farm on which the famous Allerton Oak stands, and just at the point where four ways meet, are a quantity of remains called Calder stones.

Baines' Directory, 1825

31

The Major Oak

First known as the Cockpen Tree, after the cockfighting that once took place beneath it, and later as the Queen Oak and Robin Hood's Oak, this giant tree is arguably one of the most famous in Britain. Named after Major Hayman Rooke, who made a drawing of it in 1790, it has a waistline of 10.66m (35ft) and a canopy that spreads for 28m (91.8ft). It may well have been standing for over 1,000 years and is the largest Oak in Sherwood Forest.

The tree once stood without support, whereas today a complex pattern of poles and wires support the huge branches. It was fenced off in 1975 to keep the 500,000 annual visitors from compacting the soil around its roots, the effect of which was killing the tree. It is now in good health, but the downside is that you cannot get near it. It has, in effect, become the Stonehenge of ancient trees.

The *Domesday Book* (1086) states that Sherwood Forest covered most of Nottinghamshire above the River Trent. The best parts of it survive near the village of Edwinstowe, where we find the Major Oak at Robin Hood Way. Legend has it that Robin and his men hid from their enemies inside the Major Oak. Although the tree was probably there in Robin's time, it would not have been large enough for this purpose, but the site could have been the setting for his camp.

RIGHT: The Major Oak in 1976 – my first tree portrait.

OPPOSITE: The Major Oak, 2009.

32

Sherwood Forest

NOTTINGHAMSHIRE

Contrary to popular belief, medieval Sherwood Forest was not the rich swathe of dense woodland that we might expect. Declared a royal hunting ground shortly after the Norman Conquest in 1066 (along with Windsor Forest and the New Forest amongst others), Sherwood was made up of native Birch and Oak woodland, rough grass and gorse heaths. Much of the forest was lost in the thirteenth century – popularly accepted as Robin Hood's time – as developing towns and villages used the timber for house-building, and the pastureland was cleared, but around this time the forest still covered some 100,000 acres.

Its name derives from 'Shire Wood' (wood belonging to the Shire), and it became a haven for those members of the local population who were finding it hard to make a living and were frequently in breach of forest laws for poaching. Bands of robbers congregated there and Sherwood became a dangerous place, leading to tales of outlaws (meaning 'outside of the law') and the exploits of the legendary Robin Hood.

Monarchs continued to hunt in the forest until the time of King Charles I. A fire in 1624 destroyed 4,000 acres of trees, and at the end of the seventeenth century huge lengths of oak were taken from Sherwood to construct the roof of the new St Paul's Cathedral following the Great Fire of London. By 1830, the last of the forest had been sold by the Crown into private hands, an area of which became known as 'The Dukeries' after the rich landowners who profited from its resources.

Today, the forest thrives, with its own new visitor centre, and it has recently doubled in size to 1,044 acres with the acquisition of Budby South Forest. It has been designated an SSSI (Site of Special Scientific Interest) and a National Nature Reserve, and it attracts around 500,000 visitors a year.

Romantic writers breathed new life into the forest in Victorian times, and people flocked to visit, keen to witness the setting for tales of the greenwood, including, of course, those about the legendary Robin Hood and Ivanhoe.

ABOVE: The Parliament Oak in 2009.

The Parliament Oak

CLIPSTONE, SHERWOOD FOREST, NOTTINGHAMSHIRE 10

The Parliament Oak may seem unimpressive at first glance, but it is all that remains of a tree that was once almost as large, and possibly as old, as the Major Oak. It was so named after King John who, whilst out hunting, hastily assembled a parliament there to deal with a Welsh uprising in 1212. Out of anger, permission was granted to hang 28 Welsh hostages who were being held at Nottingham Castle. They were all boys aged between 12 and 14 years old.

In 1290, Edward I also held a parliament here for two days, and the assembled lords stayed at local residences, such as King John's Palace at Clipstone, which is just over a mile away and whose ruins are still visible today.

To make this Sherwood Eden o'er again,
And these rough oaks the palms of
Paradise!

From *The Foresters*, **Alfred, Lord Tennyson,** *c.*1891

BELOW: The Parliament Oak as it was in 1910.

The legend of Robin Hood

The traditional legend of the swashbuckling champion archer places him in the reigns of King Richard I and King John, between 1189 and 1216, and there were certainly outlaws who were named Robert/Robin Hode, or Hood, living in Sherwood Forest at that time. However, one of the early ballads connects him to the reign of Edward II in the late thirteenth/early fourteenth century. By 1260, the very name Robin Hood had come to be synonymous with 'fugitives' or 'outlaws'.

The earliest written references to him appear in fourteenth-century ballads, such as *A Lytell Geste of Robin Hode*, but these may have been in circulation as an oral tradition much earlier than this. By the fifteenth century, the tales had developed into popular stories, which were related by minstrels to royalty and commoners alike, but the concept of 'stealing from the rich to give to the poor' did not become established until later, in the seventeenth century.

As with all myths and legends, the story has continued to develop and reflect the times, whenever it is retold, right up to the present day. Although it is difficult to pin the legend on one individual, it almost certainly grew from the deeds of people who were alive at the time. The real Robin Hood, however, remains as elusive to us today as he was to the Sheriff of Nottingham and his men 800 years ago.

Robin Hood's Larder

A huge Oak tree known as 'Robin Hood's Larder' once stood at Birklands, an ancient fragment of Sherwood Forest that was owned by the Crown for 600 years and is now in the hands of the Forestry Commission. First mentioned in documents in 1251, the forest takes its name from the old Viking word for 'Birch Land'.

The outlaw Robin Hood reputedly hung venison, hunted from the king's stock, inside the huge hollow trunk of the Oak tree, the purpose for which it also acquired the names 'Butcher's Oak', 'Shambles Oak' and 'The Slaughter Tree'. Large hollow Oaks were a good place to hide such stock in the days before refrigeration and the tree was doubtless used for this purpose by poachers if not by the outlaw himself.

Towards the end of the nineteenth century, some schoolgirls burnt down a large part of the tree when they were boiling a kettle. Despite heroic efforts to preserve the hulk, the tree was again damaged by fire in 1913 and it finally blew down in the great gales of 1961. Today, unfortunately, no trace of it remains.

RIGHT: Robin Hood's Larder, c.1925.

The Old Man of Calke

CALKE ABBEY, DERBYSHIRE 12 🌿🍃

The Harpur Crewe family have occupied the estate at Calke Abbey since 1622, securing a piece of old England that remains little changed in almost 400 years since they enclosed the land, built a house and founded the park. The National Trust took the house and almost 200 acres of the park into its care in 1985, since which time it has been careful not to disturb too much of the estate's old-world charm. The park's fallow deer have been fenced into one area to prevent further damage to that already inflicted upon the trees.

In the grounds stand some fine timeworn Oaks, remnants of an ancient woodland, as evidenced by the 350 species of beetle that live there. This abundance of beetle variation is found only in a habitat where the forest floor is able to become rich in decaying wood over several centuries.

Many of the Oaks predate the house, their large girths of up to 9m (29.5ft) confirming this fact. They were preserved with the enclosure of the land at a time when much of England's woodland was being felled. However, one tree in particular stands out from the crowd – an English Oak with a waistline of 10.01m (32.84ft), which is thought to be 1,200 years old or more, ranking alongside the country's sylvan elders.

Surprisingly for a tree of such stature, it had not been named, so in 2004, the year in which the Park was designated as a National Nature Reserve owing to the quality of its rare wood pasture, a competition was organised to choose a name for its most venerable Oak. A naming ceremony was held, endorsed by the Rt. Hon. Margaret Beckett MP, Secretary of State for the Environment at the time, and the tree was fittingly named 'The Old Man of Calke'. A new tree was planted near to the Old Man in the hope of creating a future ancient tree.

OPPOSITE: The Old Man of Calke at Calke Abbey in 2009.

The Bowthorpe Oak

BOWTHORPE PARK FARM, MANTHORPE, LINCOLNSHIRE 13

The Bowthorpe Oak shares the honour, along with the Fredville Oak in Kent, of being the largest girthed British Oak still alive. Its circumference measures 12.3m (40.3ft), but in 1768 it was 12m (39.5ft), so it has grown little in 240 years, indicating its decaying state. It stands in what used to be Bowthorpe Park, the tree having outlived the manor house and priory that once stood nearby in what is now private farmland. The current farm owner charges visitors a small fee, which he donates to charity, but his sheep and chickens wander freely about its hollow trunk.

Over the years, the tree has been used as a pigeon house, a cattle feeder and an extra room. One owner managed to cram 39 people inside, and declared that 13 could sit down for tea comfortably. Children from the local chapel at Manthorpe have long held their annual tea and treat in there and could have been responsible for some of the ancient graffiti visible on the inner walls of the bole.

The tree still retains a large crown, but this, too, has reduced considerably in its declining years. Bound by chains to hold the upper branches together, the Bowthorpe Oak is believed to be at least 1,000 years old.

The late possessor, George Pauncefort, Esq. (in whose family it has been for many centuries), in 1768 had it floored, with benches placed round, and a door of entrance: frequently twelve persons have dined in it with ease.

From *A Library of Wonders and Curiosities Found in Nature and Art, Science And Literature*, I Platt, 1884

*...crowds yearly flock to see
In leafy pomp the celebrated tree;
Charm'd to contemplate Nature's
    giant son,
Fed by the genial seasons as they run.*

From *A Library of Wonders and Curiosities Found in Nature and Art, Science And Literature*, I Platt, 1884

ABOVE: Ancient graffiti carved on the internal walls of the hollowed trunk, 2009.
LEFT: The Bowthorpe Oak, c.1905. Could that be a tea party going on inside?
OPPOSITE: The Bowthorpe Oak in 2009.

The Royal Oak

BOSCOBEL HOUSE, STAFFORDSHIRE 14

After King Charles I was beheaded in 1649, his eldest son, also named Charles, made a bid to claim the throne. Two years later, on 3 September 1651, at Worcester, the Civil War ended with the defeat of the Royalist forces at the hands of Oliver Cromwell and his New Model Army, and Charles became a fugitive.

Charles sought refuge at Boscobel House in Staffordshire after finding his path to Wales blocked and was sheltered there for a night by the tenants William Penderel and his wife, who guided him to an old Oak tree that stood in the grounds. Along with his companion Colonel Carlis, Charles climbed up a hen-roost ladder to hide in its branches, where they were passed food on a nut hook by the Penderels. They watched in silence as a Roundhead patrol passed directly below them, stopped to discuss Charles's arrest and then moved on in their pursuit of him.

Charles spent a further night hidden in a priest-hole in the attic of Boscobel House before finally making his escape to France in disguise, and it was not until 29 May 1660, his thirtieth birthday, that he was restored to the throne. He personally watered some acorns that he had taken from his Oak tree sanctuary and planted them at St James Palace, Westminster, near where Marlborough House now stands.

Unfortunately, the Royal Oak suffered so badly from relic hunters, who were eager to own a piece of history, that by the eighteenth century not a bit of it remained. Nearby, however, a descendant of the tree was already growing and became known as 'Son of Royal Oak'. That tree still survives, although it was badly damaged when it was struck by lightning in 2000. The following year, Prince Charles (the Prince of Wales) planted an acorn from the tree to produce a 'Grandson of Royal Oak'.

The Royal Oak is now one of the most popular pub names in England and it derives directly from this incident, which is evident from the many pub signs throughout the country that depict Charles II hiding in the tree.

The Royal Youth,
born to out-brave his Fate,
Within a neighbouring oak
maintained his state:
The faithful boughs
in kind allegiance spread
Their shelt'ring branches
round his awful head,
Twin'd their rough arms,
and thicken'd all the shade.

From *Silva*, Abraham Cowley, *c.*1680

ABOVE: Son of Boscobel Oak, 1905.

ABOVE: Cromwell and Charles II pictured by the Royal Oak in a typical pub sign, 2008.
OPPOSITE: Son of Boscobel Oak.

Oak Apple Day

Parliament had ordered the 29 of May, the King's birthday, to be for ever kept as a day of thanksgiving for our redemption from tyranny and the King's return to his Government, he entering London that day.'

Entry from *Samuel Pepys' Diary*, 1 June 1660

ABOVE: An oak apple in summer.

In 1664, the 29th May was made a public holiday by Act of Parliament. People would wear sprigs of oak with oak apples (growths containing larvae of the gall wasp) in celebration and remembrance of the day when Charles II hid from the Parliamentarian troops in the Oak tree at Boscobel. Maypole dancing took place and the streets were hung with oak boughs, supporting the view that Oak Apple Day had supplanted and, to some degree, absorbed the ancient pagan celebrations of May Day.

The holiday was formally abolished in 1859, but it is still is celebrated by the Chelsea Pensioners and lives on in some English towns, notably Upton-upon-Severn in Worcestershire, Northampton, Aston-on-Clun in Shropshire, Marsh Gibbon in Buckinghamshire, Great Wishford in Wiltshire and Membury in Devon. At Oxford and Cambridge Universities, a traditional toast to celebrate Oak Apple Day is still drunk in some halls.

The Shelton Oak

SHREWSBURY, SHROPSHIRE 15

The Welsh hero and freedom fighter Owain Glyndwr had stomached enough of the English bullying tactics towards his country and in 1400 launched a partially effective guerrilla war against his oppressors, known as 'The Welsh Revolt'.

On 21 July 1403, Glyndwr is said to have approached Shrewsbury with his growing band of men to join his ally the Duke of Northumberland against Henry IV in the Battle of Shrewsbury, but on arrival he found his route blocked by the King's troops. Whether Glyndwr was there at the time is contested, but legend has him climbing the Shelton Oak three miles from the ensuing battle to inspect proceedings. From this vantage point, when he saw that the duke had not joined his son Hotspur in the fray, Glyndwr decided not to proceed to the fight and retreated to Oswestry. Hotspur was killed and the King was victorious, although badly wounded when an arrow struck him in the face.

Glyndwr fought on for many years, but Henry died in 1413, and his son and successor Henry V acted more graciously towards the Welsh. After 1412 nothing is known about Glyndwr, but he was never captured or betrayed. Legend says he sleeps in Castle Cave in Gwent and will return to establish Welsh independence with his warriors once England is degenerate. Some would say he is long overdue. He was the last Welshman to hold the title 'Prince of Wales'.

In 1884, the Shelton Oak was described as 'now in a complete state of decay, and hollow, even in the larger ramifications' by I Platt in *A Library of Wonders and Curiosities Found in Nature and Art, Science and Literature*, and it was given a waist measurement of 7.64m (25ft). By 1940, it was dead, and the stump was removed in the 1950s to accommodate improvements to the junction of the Welshpool road and the A5 where the tree stood.

Another oak associated with Glyndwr, known as *Ceubren yr Elbyl* ('The Hollow Tree of the Devil') stood at Nannau Park, Gwynedd. Around 1406, he is said to have imprisoned his mortally wounded cousin Hywel Sele (a sympathiser of the English) within its hollow trunk and left him there to die.

ABOVE: The Shelton Oak, c.1900.

44

The Midland Oak

The centuries-old Midland Oak, also known as the Lillington Oak after the village in which it stood, long laid claim to mark the very heart of England. Lillington, which was subsumed as a parish into neighbouring Leamington Spa in 1890, was an ancient village that predated the Domesday Book of 1086 in which it is mentioned.

However, the tree fell and was replaced in the 1950s with an Oak grown from an acorn found nearby. That tree was then replaced in 1988 from another local acorn and still stands today, surviving major landscaping works, which were undertaken to alleviate flooding in the immediate area, and upholding the lineage.

A commemorative plaque, which was erected beside the tree, affirms the claim of it being at the very centre of England, but this fact has long been disputed. Not 12 miles to the northwest at Meriden stands a 500-year-old stone cross, with an inscription making the same claim. Meriden's other claims to fame include having a church dedicated to St Lawrence, supposedly founded by Lady Godiva, and hosting the site of the former Triumph motorcycle factory, which closed in 1983 and was demolished. It is now the site of a housing estate.

In 2002, Ordnance Survey set out to accurately determine Britain's geographical centres and named Lindley Hall Farm in Leicestershire as England's – some 15 miles to the southeast of Lillington. Between Blair Atholl and Dalwhinnie in Perthshire was named as Scotland's central point, while a spot near Cwmystwyth, Devil's Bridge, Ceredigion, was given as that of Wales. However, their calculations included offshore islands as opposed to just the mainland, and what with coastal erosion providing an ever-changing shape to the country, Lillington would do well to hang on to its claims for some time to come.

ABOVE: The Midland Oak in 1938.

ABOVE: The Midland Oak in 1905.

The Battle Oak

MORTIMER'S CROSS, HEREFORDSHIRE 17

The Battle of Mortimer's Cross, one of the decisive battles of the Wars of the Roses, was fought on 2 February 1461 between Edward, Duke of York (later Edward IV), for the Yorkists, and Owen Tudor for the House of Lancaster. The latter was defeated and later beheaded on that same day in Hereford.

It is quite possible that this tree was standing at the time of the battle; it was certainly an ancient tree when this photograph was taken over a century ago. The characteristic signs of ageing are all present – the substantial hollowing trunk, gnarled bark, and the loss of its upper branches – a survival technique that aids longevity. Relics from the battle have been ploughed up in the fields around the tree, including bridle bits, stirrups and fragments of iron.

On the first edition Ordnance Survey map from 1885, the tree is referred to as the 'Gospel Oak'. Many old trees were called Gospel Oaks, relating to the time when the gospels were preached from beneath their mighty shade. The tree was cut down in recent years, but a new Oak has been planted in its place.

No longer Earl of March, but Duke of York:
The next degree is England's royal throne;
For King of England shalt thou be proclaim'd
In every borough as we pass along;
And he that throws not up his cap for joy
Shall for the fault make forfeit of his head.
King Edward, valiant Richard, Montague,
Stay we no longer, dreaming of renown,
But sound the trumpets, and about our task.

From *Henry VI*, William Shakespeare

ABOVE: The replacement Battle Oak with the site of the battlefield beyond, 2008.

LEFT: The Battle Oak in 1906.

The Holgate Oak

KINGSLAND, HEREFORDSHIRE 18

Not far from Battle Oak stands the Holgate Oak. In 1760, the area around it was known as 'Howgate', and later 'Holgate', meaning 'gate in the hole', in reference to the tree, which around this time was thought to have died. Someone had the idea of knocking through the hollow trunk to frame a gateway to Holgate Farm, which is visible behind the tree in the archive photograph. Shortly afterwards the 'dead' tree sprang back to life, and miraculously it still survives to this day in fine condition – my visit in the autumn of 2008 showed the Holgate Oak rich with acorns. The farm also doubles as a bed and breakfast – I stayed in the room top right in the photograph – and enjoyed a fine breakfast.

A girth measuring 6.22m (20.4ft) suggests that the tree could be 450 years old, considering it was already hollow some 250 years ago. The current tenant farmers take particular pride in the tree and have rebuilt the picket gate and fence, ensuring that the scene has barely changed since the archive photograph was taken around 100 years ago.

*Solitary trees,
if they grow at all,
grow strong.*

Winston Churchill

ABOVE: The tree in 2008.

RIGHT: The Holgate Oak, c. 1910.

47

The Queen's Oak
POTTERSPURY, NORTHAMPTONSHIRE 19

According to folklore, King Edward IV met Elizabeth Woodville beneath the shade of this tree on 13 April 1464. Just 18 days later they were married. As Queen, Elizabeth bore two sons, Edward and Richard, who were made famous by Shakespeare as 'The Princes in the Tower'. In 1483, their uncle Richard III had them taken to the Tower of London and they were never seen again. The general consensus was that Richard arranged for them to be killed to eliminate any threat to his ascension to the throne.

The Queen's Oak was found to have a girth of 6.83m (22.4ft) in 1879, its hollow trunk capable of accommodating 18 people. Henry Newton, the co-founder of Windsor and Newton artist materials, planted acorns from the tree at his neighbouring estate of Potterspury Lodge in the mid-nineteenth century.

Woodman, spare that tree!
Touch not a single bough!
In youth it sheltered me,
And I'll protect it now.
T'was my forefather's hand
That placed it near his cot;
There, woodman, let it stand,
Thy axe shall harm it not.

George Pope Morris (1802–1864)

BELOW: The Queen's Oak, *c*.1907. The archive photograph shows the tree to be in good health, which continued until 1994 when it caught fire. For three years the Oak lived on, producing foliage on one branch, until it finally gave up the ghost in August 1997.

The Gospel Oak
POLSTEAD, SUFFOLK 20

The village of Polstead is probably known best for the notorious 'Red Barn Murder' that took place there in 1824. Maria Marten was found buried in the barn by her father almost a year after her death. Aged just 26, she had been shot and stabbed by her lover, local farmer William Corder, who was later hanged for the crime at Bury St Edmunds.

A manuscript bound with Corder's own skin recounts the story of his trial and can still be seen in the museum in Bury St Edmunds. Maria lies buried in the graveyard of the twelfth-century St Mary's church, her tombstone long gone – chipped away by successive souvenir hunters.

However, of equal interest is the Gospel Oak, which stood with a girth of 9.7m (31.8ft) in the grounds of Polstead Hall next to the churchyard. Legend points its origins to St Cedd, a seventh-century bishop, who is thought to have preached a sermon beneath the tree in 653 and is rumoured to have planted it.

Cedd died from plague 11 years later, but an annual service was held consecutively beneath its branches on the first Sunday of August for more than a millennium until its collapse in 1953, outliving its benefactor by 1,300 years. A descendant of the tree grows nearby, where the service is still held.

Should you see me at the point of death,
carry me under the shade of an oak,
and I promise you I shall recover.

Jean-Jacques Rousseau (1712–1778)

RIGHT: The Gospel Oak, c.1910.

The Old Oak

ROSS-ON-WYE, HEREFORDSHIRE 21

This great Oak stands on a flood plain, which is known as 'Horse Shoe Bend' and is surrounded by the River Wye on three sides. It was previously in the company of several other old Oaks, but they are now gone. Tradition holds that it was planted in the reign of Henry VIII, making it close to 500 years old, but a girth of 10.9m (35.7ft) suggests an even greater age than that. The middle section has completely rotted away, giving the impression of two trees; an iron rod that clamps the two parts together is the only remaining clue that it was originally one.

ABOVE: The Old Oak Tree in 2008.
BELOW: The Old Oak Tree, 1914.

The Lassington Oak
GLOUCESTER, GLOUCESTERSHIRE 22

ABOVE: The Lassington Oak in 2008.

LASSINGTON, *a parish in the lower division of the hundred of Dudstone, county Gloucester, three miles N.W. of Gloucester, its post town. The parish, which is of small extent, is bounded on the N. and E. by the River Leadon. The Hereford and Gloucester canal here crosses a branch of the River Severn, and joins the main branch at Gloucester. In the neighbourhood both rivers are crossed by the same bridge, and near it is a large oak tree called 'Lassington Oak'.*

Extract from *National Gazetteer*, 1868

ABOVE: The Lassington Oak in 1907.

A fallen, broken hollow trunk is all that remains of this once mighty Oak. Its blackened hulk shows that it was set on fire recently. It lies in Lassington Wood, which has been designated a Site of Special Scientific Interest (SSSI), and it is marked on the first-edition Ordnance Survey Map of 1882. By 1907, the tree was already in need of support to hold up its huge branches, and it eventually fell within living memory.

The name of the tree lives on with the Lassington Oak Morris Men, who named themselves after it when they formed in 1977. A new tree, which was planted by its side, now flourishes.

The Newland Oak
NEWLAND, GLOUCESTERSHIRE 23

Here is the earliest known photograph of the Newland Oak, which was taken around 1900. The tree was probably 1,000 years old by then, a remnant of the nearby Forest of Dean, but by this time it sat alone in a field at Sprouts Farm.

It is the second largest girthed English Oak ever recorded, after the Cowthorpe Oak (see page 28), measuring 13.25m (43.47ft) in 1906 and reaching a massive 13.72m (45ft) by 1950. Five years later, in May 1955, the tree collapsed under the weight of heavy snow and retained only one live branch.

To add insult to injury, it was set alight by vandals in 1970, and this marked the end of its life, but the trunk continues to rot next to a direct descendant, which was grown from one of its own acorns and was planted in 1964.

BELOW: The Newland Oak today.
BOTTOM: The Newland Oak in 1904.

Merlin's Oak

Merlin's Oak once stood on the corner of Oak Lane and Priory Street in Carmarthen. According to legend, the town was the birthplace of Merlin, the wizard of Arthurian folklore, and this is based on the premise that the origin of the name Carmarthen, or *Caerfyrddin*, might have derived from *Myrddin*, the Welsh name for Merlin. He is said to have made a prophecy regarding the old Oak tree:

When Merlin's Tree shall tumble down,
Then shall fall Carmarthen Town.

In the early nineteenth century, a local man apparently tried to poison the tree with the intention of preventing people from meeting under it, but the Oak survived and is believed to have lived on until 1856.

The legend of Merlin's prophecy was taken so seriously that in later years the gnarled rotting stump was bound in iron and concrete in a desperate attempt to stave off the predicted fall of Carmarthen. The last fragments of the tree were finally removed in 1978 and are now displayed in the Civic Hall of Carmarthen. Around this time, the town suffered terrible floods, so Merlin's prophecy could, in some part, have been realised.

RIGHT Merlin's Oak, still standing in Priory Road in 1936.

OLD OAK CARMARTHEN   87418

When Priory Oak shall tumble down
Then will fall Carmarthen Town

Merlin's Prophecy

Queen Elizabeth's Oak

HATFIELD PARK, HERTFORDSHIRE 25

Queen Elizabeth I spent most of her childhood at the royal palace of Hatfield House in Hertfordshire. She was reputedly sitting beneath this once great pollarded tree in the park – eating an apple or reading the Bible, or both (take your pick) – when a messenger arrived hotfoot from London with news of her sister Mary's death, heralding her accession to the throne on 17 November 1558. Her first words after hearing the news were allegedly:

The top of hope supposed the root
  upreared shall be,
And fruitless all their grafted guile,
  as shortly ye shall see.
The dazzled eyes with pride,
  which great ambition blinds,
Shall be unsealed by worthy wights
  whose foresight falsehood finds.

The Doubt of Future Foes,
Queen Elizabeth I (1533–1603)

This is the Lord's doing,
and it is marvelous in our eyes.

King George III visited Hatfield House in 1800, and when Queen Victoria went there in 1846 she took an acorn from the Oak. It is quite literally on its last legs in this photograph, propped up with struts and bound with iron. The dead remnants of the old tree were finally removed on 17 November 1978, exactly 420 years after Elizabeth I's coronation day. They remain in storage on site until a suitable use can be decided for them. In 1985, Queen Elizabeth II symbolically planted a new Oak tree in its place.

RIGHT: Queen Elizabeth's Oak, Hatfield Park, c.1935.

The Minchenden Oak

SOUTHGATE, GREATER LONDON 26

An ancient pollarded sessile oak, which is thought to be a survivor of the ancient Forest of Middlesex, stands in Minchenden Oak Gardens. These were formerly the grounds of Minchenden House, one of the area's great estates, which was built around 1747 by John Nicholl. The tree was already of a substantial size in his time, and it became known as the Chandos Oak during the occupancy of the Chandos family, who bought the estate from him. In 1773, Dr James Beattie knew the tree by this name, and in 1826 an engraving of it appeared in Jacob George Strutt's *Sylva Britannica* under the same name, when it measured 4.8m (15.75ft) in girth at 0.9m (3ft) from the ground. By 1873, Edward Walford reported that its spread was 'no less than 126 feet, and it is still growing'.

ABOVE: The Minchenden Oak, Southgate, c. 1940.
BELOW: The Minchenden Oak, Southgate, 2008.

The mansion was demolished in 1853, but a smaller house, Minchenden Lodge, was built soon afterwards and it still stands nearby. Minchenden Oak Gardens were opened in 1934 as a place of remembrance, and the tree now bears their name and has a girth of 6m (19.6ft). It is believed to be around 800 years old.

In the graveyard of the adjacent Christ Church stands another splendid Oak with a girth of 5m (16.4ft), which bears more than a passing resemblance to its distinguished neighbour.

...its boughs bending to the earth, with almost artificial regularity of form, and equidistance from each other, give it the appearance of a gigantic tent. A magnificent living canopy, impervious to the day.

From *Sylva Brittanica*, J G Strutt, 1826

Epping Forest
ESSEX

At 6,000 acres, Epping Forest is officially the largest open space in London. Nestled between Greater London and Essex, it was thought to have been designated a Royal Forest by Henry II during the twelfth century. In the eighteenth century, the forest became notorious for highwaymen. Of particular note was Dick Turpin, who had a hideout there and reportedly once roasted an old woman over a fire to procure her valuables.

Attempts to enclose the forest caused uproar amongst the locals, who were keen to preserve their forest lopping rights for fuel and animal grazing, and in 1878 the Epping Forest Act was passed, which not only saved the forest but ensured similar acts of enclosure would not take place elsewhere in the country. The forest was taken into the care of the City of London Corporation, which still conserves it to this day 'for the recreation and enjoyment of the people'.

Mighty oaks from tiny acorns grow.
Fourteenth-century proverb

RIGHT: Mature Beech and Oak at Amesbury Banks, Epping Forest, 1910.

The Pulpit Oak

EPPING FOREST, ESSEX 27

At over 5m (16.4ft) in girth, the Pulpit Oak is the largest of the species in Epping Forest. Its appearance quite obviously gave it its name, but the tree could well have been used as a Gospel Oak, a board having been fixed at the top of its bole to stand on.

The tree is thought to have been a rallying point for commoners fighting the enclosure of Knighton Wood where it grows. However, they were unsuccessful and the wood was incorporated into private gardens, but it was returned to the forest in 1930 and now contains the area's largest concentration of veteran trees, including many pollarded Oaks and Hornbeams.

ABOVE: The Pulpit Oak, as it was in 1930.
LEFT: The Pulpit Oak in 2011.

Harold's Oak

EPPING FOREST, ESSEX 28

Harold Godwinson succeeded his father as the powerful Earl of Wessex in 1053. He became King of England on 5 January 1066, which angered William, Duke of Normandy, who swore that Harold had promised the throne to him. Later that year, William invaded England, landing with an army of 7,000 men at Pevensey in Sussex. Harold was in Yorkshire defeating Harold Hardrada, a Viking contender to the throne, but hastily made his way south. His tired, battered army set up camp on Senlac Hill near Hastings, where they met William in a pitched battle that ended in defeat for Harold, marking the end of the Saxon dynasty in England.

Confusion reigns as to Harold's final resting place, but a strong contender is Waltham Abbey, consecrated by Harold in 1060 and a stone's throw from High Beech at Epping Forest where 'Harold's Oak' once stood. Like him, the tree is long gone but these early photographs show the remains of its large stump.

ABOVE: Harold's Oak, c.1900.
BELOW: Harold's Oak, c.1910, with Victoria's Oak, which also died, nearby.

The Fairlop Oak
HAINAULT FOREST, ESSEX 29

The celebrated Fairlop Oak stood on a clearing in Hainault Forest, in an area known as the King's Wood, with a girth of 9m (29.5ft) in 1748. Queen Anne is reputed to have visited the tree earlier that century, but it was famous not only for its great age and size.

In the early 1720s, a local block and pump maker by the name of Daniel Day collected annual rent from his tenants on the first Friday of July from beneath its branches, accompanied by friends, with whom he would feast on bacon and beans. By 1725, others

To Hainault Forest Queen Anne did ride,
And saw the old oak standing by her side,
And as she looked at it from bottom to top,
She said to her Court, it should be at
*   Fairlop.*

From *Come, Come my Boys*, sung at the Fairlop Fair

BELOW: *The Fairlop Oak*, drawn by Dayes, engraved by W Owen, 1789.

had joined the gathering and stalls were set up selling wares. There was entertainment in the form of bands, puppet shows and acrobats. None went without cover from the tree's gargantuan shade, which was said to cover an acre of ground. To mark his arrival, Day, who was known as 'Good Day', had wheels attached to a frigate, which was drawn by six horses. He served the traditional feast from within the Oak's hollow trunk, and the Fairlop Fair gained a reputation for being a well-organised affair.

However, in 1736, there were prosecutions for illegal gaming and liquor sales. By 1750, the fair had grown to such an extent that it was reported to have hosted 100,000 visitors. The year 1765 saw people meeting in a 'riotous and tumultuous manner' and the fair was eventually banned in 1793. However, the following year heralded its reappearance, and it continued to be held for another century.

In the mid-1760s, a large branch fell from the Oak tree, and Day had it made into a coffin. He died in 1767, aged 84, and was buried in it. By 1790, Fairlop, as the tree was affectionately known, was firmly into its period of decay. A plaque on it read: 'All good foresters are requested not to hurt this old tree, a plaster having lately been applied to its wounds'. In June 1805, it was inadvertently set on fire by picknickers who cooked inside the cavernous trunk. On Fairday in 1813, a boy was paid by a visiting gentleman to climb the tree and pick its last sprig of leaves, and, finally, in February 1820, the Fairlop Oak was blown down in a storm.

However, this was not the end of the story. Much of the timber was salvaged and made into furniture. A lot of the timber was bought by a Mr Seabrooke, who built St Pancras church on the Euston Road in London. The pulpit (pictured below) was made from it and is your best chance of glimpsing the remnants of this once great tree.

In 1850, 3,000 acres of the King's Wood were felled and turned into farmland. A century later, a new Oak was planted in honour of Fairlop and it can be seen on a roundabout at Fullwell Cross.

RIGHT: The Pulpit at St Pancras Church, 2010.

Turpin's Oak

EAST FINCHLEY, LONDON 30

Turpin's Oak grew on the corner of Oak Lane (which took its name from the tree) and the High Road in East Finchley, in the garden of Hilton House. Its huge trunk gave good cover for highwaymen lying in wait to ambush travellers as they crossed the notoriously dangerous Finchley Common on the Great North Road. Coach drivers would frequently shoot at the tree when passing to deter any would-be robbers, and when it was finally cut down in 1956, the trunk was found to be riddled with musket shots.

Dick Turpin himself was reputed to have sheltered by the tree whilst waiting with his partner Tom King to rob the mail coach in 1724, although it could have been named after owners of the same name. Although he was England's most famous highwayman, Turpin was not, in fact, the dashing, swashbuckling hero that he is generally believed to be, but a cold and ruthless killer who did not think twice about torturing his victims to gain their valuables. It was not until his death in 1739 that he even showed some of the gallantry for which he became famous. On his way to the gibbet he chatted and joked with the crowds that had gathered and according to an account in the York Courant of his execution:

…with undaunted courage looked about him, and after speaking a few words to the topsman, he threw himself off the ladder and expired in about five minutes.

Other famous highwaymen included Jack Sheppard, who was captured in 1724 at a farmhouse on Finchley Common, having escaped from a prison cell in Newgate to which he was promptly returned. Later that year he was hanged at Tyburn, the execution attracting crowds of up to 200,000 people, one-third of London's population at the time, such was the fame of his exploits.

Finchley Common was long noted for its highwaymen, and there is a tree still standing known as Turpin's Oak.

From *The National Gazetteer of Great Britain and Ireland*, 1868

ABOVE: Turpin's Oak, from the *The Illustrated London News*, 25 May 1850.

ABOVE: Turpin's Oak, c. 1905.

The Elfin Oak

KENSINGTON GARDENS, LONDON 31

This wonderfully eccentric sculpture can be found in Kensington Gardens, next to the Princess Diana Memorial Playground.

The 800-year-old, six-metre-tall hollow trunk originally came from Richmond Park, London, where it had suffered storm damage, and was moved to central London as part of George Lansbury's appeal for public improvements in the city in 1928. Lady Fortescue commissioned the illustrator Ivor Innes to carve and paint 'little people', including small animals, fairies, gnomes and elves, as though they were living in the bark. The sculpture took two years to complete, and Innes continued to maintain it for the next 40 years.

All the characters were named, including Wookey the witch, Huckleberry the gnome, Grumples and Groodles the elves, and Brownie, Dinkie, Rumplelocks and Hereandthere, seen stealing eggs from a crow's nest. In 1930, the sculptor's wife Elsie wrote a book entitled *The Elfin Oak*, recounting stories about all the characters who were featured on the tree.

The tree fell into decay but was saved by the comedian Spike Milligan, a lifelong fan, who successfully led an appeal for funds to restore it in 1996. He carried out much of the work himself, with some help from his friends, but the tree was vandalised, so now it stands protected within a huge birdcage.

In 1997, the tree was added to the List of Buildings of Special Architectural or Historic Interest and was awarded Grade II status, affording it the protection it needs.

ABOVE: The Elfin Oak, c. 1930.

ABOVE: The Elfin Oak caged in 2010.

ABOVE: Carved images on the Elfin Oak.

Richmond Park

LONDON

At 2,500 acres, Richmond Park is London's largest Royal Park and boasts the city's finest collection of ancient pollarded Oaks, many of them aged between 400 and 700 years old.

Originally known as the Manor of Sheen in the reign of Edward I, it was renamed Richmond Park in Henry VII's time. When Charles I moved to Richmond Palace to escape the plague in 1625, he stocked it with deer, enclosing the area in 1637 to prevent the herd from wandering, much to the annoyance of the local people. Around 650 Red and Fallow Deer still roam freely in the park.

In the late seventeenth century, a survey was carried out of the trees and it recorded 2,000 Oaks 'rotten and not much use for anything other than firewood'. However, as many as 1,000 of these trees survive as the great veterans we see today.

Copyright   The Park. Richmond   10648

ABOVE: Looking down the hill towards Ham Dip Pond, c.1905.

RIGHT: Ancient pollard Oaks marking the old boundary before the park was enclosed.

Martin's Oak

ABOVE: *In Richmond Park* by John Martin, 1850.

ABOVE: Martin's Oak in 2009.

An avenue of Hornbeam trees leads from Pembroke Lodge towards Ham Gate, at the end of which stands Martin's Oak, so named after the romantic artist John Martin who painted it. Born in Newcastle in 1789, he moved to London in 1806 to develop his art, hoping to make a living from it. However, he was robbed of almost everything he owned en route and arrived in the city almost destitute.

Martin spent much of his time painting London's suburban – but then rural – landscapes. One such painting, entitled *In Richmond Park*, clearly depicts in watercolour the tree that took his name (above). The painting now hangs for all to see in The Victoria and Albert Museum in London.

At an estimated 750 years old, Martin's Oak is amongst the park's oldest and still stands proud with a girth of around 7m (23ft). It has clearly lost some major branches since Martin's painting was executed, but this is just a normal part of the Oak's ageing process.

OPPOSITE: Richmond Park, Ham Dip Pond, in 2009.

Windsor Great Park

Windsor Great Park is set in 5,000 acres on the border that divides Berkshire from Surrey, nestled in countryside between Windsor and Ascot. Originally reserved as a hunting ground for William the Conqueror, who started building the famous castle there in the eleventh century, the park still hosts a large semi-wild deer herd, a reminder of its original purpose.

The park is a remnant of the once vast Windsor Forest, which stretched for another 20 miles to the southwest. The Crouch Oak in Addlestone (see page 86) previously marked the boundary. There are several hundred ancient Oaks in the park, some of which are believed to date back to its inception. The very act of William's draconian measures to secure hunting grounds for his own pleasure, which no doubt presented some hardships to the local populace of the time, has, in effect, 1,000 years later preserved some of Britain's finest examples of ancient trees.

ABOVE: Ancient Oaks, also known as Dodders, in the Cranbourne area of the Great Park in 2008.
RIGHT: *Windsor Forest* by Richard Wilson (1714–1782) at Anglesey Abbey.

ABOVE: The Watch Oak, Windsor Great Park, from *Picturesque Europe*, *c.* 1876.

Herne the Hunter

WINDSOR GREAT PARK, BERKSHIRE 33

Herne the Hunter's most recent replacement Oak, photographed below in 2008, was planted in 1906 by command of Edward VII. The original tree was cut down in 1796, being dead, and its name was transferred to a nearby Oak, which, in turn, was blown down in 1863 and replaced with a new one by Queen Victoria in 1866.

LEFT: Herne the Hunter.

*There is an old tale goes that Herne
   the Hunter,
Sometime a keeper here in Windsor Forest,
Doth all the winter-time, at still midnight,
Walk round about an oak,
   with great ragg'd horns;
And there he blasts the tree,
   and takes cattle,
And makes milch-kine yield blood,
   and shakes a chain
In a most hideous and dreadful manner.
You have heard of such a spirit,
   and well you know
The superstitious idle-headed eld
Received and did deliver to our age,
This tale of Herne the Hunter for a truth.*

From *The Merry Wives of Windsor*, William Shakespeare

LEFT: Herne the Hunter's replacement Oak, 2008, located in Home Park – a private area inaccessible to the public.

The Conqueror's Oak

WINDSOR GREAT PARK, BERKSHIRE 34

Also known as 'The King Oak', this tree is a contender for one of Windsor Great Park's oldest specimens. I was taken to see it by Bill Cathcart of the Crown Estate (opposite) who told me it is known as 'The Conqueror's Oak'. Standing by the roadside at Forest Gate, it was almost certainly there at the time of the conqueror and was later most probably used as a hanging tree – at 9.34m (30.64ft) in girth, you would be hard pushed to find a better candidate.

During the First World War, the Canadian Forestry Corps were stationed at Windsor and claimed to have cut down the famous Oak for timber as part of the war effort, but if you delve deeper into the forest, in an overgrown thicket that was formerly a great avenue lined with Chestnut trees, many of which survive, stands the 'true' Conqueror's Oak. Long dead, the great hulk still cuts a fine figure and can be identified on the early maps that firmly place it there.

ABOVE: Engraving of the Conqueror's Oak from *Picturesque Europe*, c.1876.

OPPOSITE: Forest Gate contender in 2008.

ABOVE: The 'true' Conqueror's Oak in 2009

We lunched in it: it would accommodate at least 20 persons with standing room; and 10 or 12 might sit down comfortably to dinner. I think, at Willis's and in Guildhall, I have danced a quadrille in a smaller space.

Professor Burnet, 2 September 1829

The largest and oldest of all is reputed to have lived a thousand years, and to have been a favourite tree with William the Conqueror, whose name it bears. It is quite hollow, as may be seen, and the space within its trunk is full seven feet in diameter.

From *Picturesque Europe*, c.1870

Offa's Oak

WINDSOR GREAT PARK, BERKSHIRE 35 🌿

King Offa (757–796) was a Saxon king of Mercia (the Midlands) with a lust for power that eventually led him to rule most of England south of the Humber. He is most famously remembered for constructing Offa's Dyke, a huge earthwork that runs almost the entire length of the Welsh border and marked the western extent of his power. His bloodthirsty temperament finally backfired on his son Ecgfrith, as Offa eliminated all opposition to his future heir's crown. Ecgfrith died only 141 days after his succession, according to Alcuin, a ninth-century scholar, 'for the blood his father shed to secure the kingdom for his son'.

Sitting between the two 1,000-year-old Conqueror Oaks mentioned previously (see page 72), Offa's Oak is believed to be even older. The huge trunk split into three a long time ago – one section lies fallen at 90 degrees to the others – but the tree still thrives and produces a great green crown in summer.

Ted Green, one of Britain's foremost experts on ancient trees and Windsor Park in particular, named it, believing that it could have been a sapling back in Offa's time, making the tree the oldest Oak in the park at somewhere approaching 1,500 years old.

ABOVE: King Offa raises St Alban's head in 793. His bones were reputedly discovered due to a star, which was located over the place of martyrdom.

BELOW: Offa's Oak in 2009.

The Victoria Oak

WINDSOR FOREST, BERKSHIRE 36

In 1756, the civil engineer John Smeaton was commissioned to design a lighthouse on the Eddystone rocks, 14 miles southwest of Plymouth, Devon. He set about the task by improving on the two previous constructions, which had both fallen into the sea. The first was destroyed with its creator, Henry Winstanley, during a violent storm in 1703; the second after a fire in which the duty keeper, Henry Hall, swallowed seven ounces of molten lead as he was looking up. Nobody believed his tale until his death a few days later, when doctors found the lump of metal in his stomach; it is now on display in the Edinburgh Museum.

Apparently, inspiration for the design of his lighthouse came to Smeaton when he noticed the elasticity and strength of the Victoria Oak in Windsor Forest during a storm. He noted how it rose from a swelling base with an elegant concave curve, and then formed a cylinder, which again swelled at the boughs.

He settled on a hollow construction using 1,493 interlocking blocks of stone to emulate the rings of a hollow tree, allowing the lighthouse to sway in the wind, much as an Oak would, and to withstand everything the elements could throw at it.

There Smeaton's new lighthouse remained at Eddystone rocks until 1882 when it was dismantled and reconstructed on Plymouth Hoe, due to some cracks appearing in the bedrock beneath it. Unlike the Victoria Oak, it still stands and became the blueprint for most future lighthouses.

The Victoria Oak, Windsor Forest.

ABOVE: The Victoria Oak, Windsor Forest, c.1850.

*Me father was the keeper of
    the Eddystone Light,
And he slept with a mermaid
    one fine night
Out of this union there came three,
A porpoise and a porgy,
    and the other was me!*

Sea shanty (Anon.)

LEFT: The Eddystone Lighthouse in 1882.

The Wilberforce Oak

KESTON, KENT 37

The Wilberforce Oak lies in the grounds of Holwood House, the home of the former British Prime Minister William Pitt the Younger. The tree was named after Pitt's friend William Wilberforce, the anti-slavery campaigner, who was a frequent visitor. The pair would sit together under the tree putting the world to rights. On one such visit, Wilberforce made the following vow, which is recorded for posterity in his diary of 1788 as follows:

At length, I well remember after a conversation with Mr Pitt in the open air at the root of an old tree at Holwood, just above the steep descent into the vale of Keston, I resolved to give notice on a fit occasion in the House of Commons of my intention to bring forward the abolition of the slave trade.

After many setbacks, a bill was eventually passed in 1833 abolishing slavery in the British Empire, just a few days before Wilberforce died.

The Wilberforce Oak was blown down during a storm in 1991 and is commemorated by a seat, which was engraved in 1862 with the reformer's aforementioned famous diary entry.

There grewe an aged Tree on the greene,
A goodly Oake sometime had it bene,
With armes full strong
   and largely displayed,
But of their leaves they were disarayde:
The bodie bigge, and mightily pight,
Thoroughly rooted,
   and of wonderous hight:
Whilome had bene the King of the field,
And mochell mast
   to the husband did yielde,
And with his nuts larded many swine.
But now the gray mosse marred his rine,
His bared boughes
   were beaten with stormes,
His toppe was bald, & wasted with wormes,
His honor decayed, his braunches sere.

February from *The Shepheardes Calender*, **Edmund Spenser (1552–1599)**

LEFT: This photograph records the visit of the first black Anglican bishop, Samuel Crowther, and his friends to the Wilberforce Oak in 1873. By this time it had become a significant place of pilgrimage and symbolised the abolition of the slave trade.

The tree of freedom is the British Oak.

From *Rejected Addresses*, **Lord Byron (1788–1824)**

OPPOSITE: The Wilberforce Oak, *c.*1873.

Knole Park

The ancestral seat of the Sackville family since 1603 and one of the largest baronial mansions in England, Knole Park was presented to the National Trust in 1946, but most of the grounds still belong to the Sackvilles. The house stands in extensive parkland, which covers about 1,000 acres and is nearly six miles in circumference.

During the great storm of October 1987, about 70 per cent of the trees in the park were lost in just one night. All of the ancient trees illustrated in the following pages were destroyed, being particularly vulnerable to the high winds due to their great age. However, the storm also presented an opportunity, and over the next five years, on the initiative of the 6th Lord Sackville, the 1,000 acres were replanted at a cost of £1 million, of which Sackville family trusts paid one half and grants contributed the other.

Knole was the setting of Virginia Woolf's novel *Orlando* (1928), which was inspired by her friend and lover Vita Sackville-West, who lived there, and the original manuscript remains on display. It was also the setting for Sackville-West's novel *The Edwardians* (1930), and her epic poem *The Land* (1926), which won the Hawthornden Prize in 1927.

RIGHT: Deer at Knole Park in 2009.

The 'Oldest Oak in England'

KNOLE PARK, KENT 38 ❧

This venerable old beast lays claim to be the 'Oldest Oak in England', according to the title of the archive photograph (right), and, although being of obvious stature, it would surely find some other contenders to the title within the pages of this book.

In the photograph, however, it is clearly approaching the end of its natural life, as evidenced by a plethora of posts and the iron banding put in place in an attempt to hold the hollow trunk together. The great storm of 1987 put paid to that work, as this tree finally came down along with many other ancient trees in the park. The fallen trunks and rotting stumps have been left where they fell as a testament to the old sentinels that stood there, and they still provide homes for countless species of wildlife. Some invertebrates are found only in the habitat of rotting Oaks and nowhere else.

ABOVE: The 'Oldest Oak in England' at Knole Park, 1895.

LEFT: A fallen Oak at Knole Park, 2010.

The Seven Oaks

SEVENOAKS, KENT 39

The town of Sevenoaks in Kent probably took its name from the Saxon word *Seouenaca*, after a seventh-century chapel in Knole Park, rather than from the seven Oaks for which it is now famous. The trees in this photograph stand on the northern edge of the Vine Cricket Ground and predate those that were planted in 1902 to mark the coronation of Edward VII, six of which came crashing down in the hurricane of 1987. These were replaced, in turn, by yet another seven Oaks, so there are now eight standing. I wonder if they will change the name of the town to 'Eightoaks'?

Flow down the woods
and stipple leaves with sun.

From *The Land*, Vita Sackville-West, 1926

Floreant Septum Quercus
(May the Seven Oaks Flourish)
Sevenoaks town motto

BELOW: The Seven Oaks in 1900.

The Lingfield Oak
LINGFIELD, KENT 40

The Lingfield Oak remains in good health and still holds its place in the centre of the village. Hollow-trunked and propped at one bough, it cuts a fine figure with a girth of 6.94m (22.77ft), and it could date to the same period as St Peter's Cross, which was built as a boundary marker in 1473. Indeed, the tree may have marked the local boundary before the cross was built, and it is thought to have been used as a hanging tree.

The Cage beside it was added in 1773 and was used as a lock-up for the detention of petty offenders until 1882. A smaller Oak stands behind it and was grown from one of the old Oak's acorns, as were some of the trees at the nearby Lingfield Nature Reserves.

This cross was built circa 1473 to designate the boundaries of Puttenden and Billeshurst Manor. The Cage for the detention of petty offenders added in 1773 was last used in 1882 to detain poachers.

Engraving on the south face of The Cage and St Peter's Cross

ABOVE: The Lingfield Oak and the Old Cage, c.1920.

LEFT: The Lingfield Oak in 2009.

The Sidney Oak

PENSHURST PARK, KENT 41

Standing in the grounds of Penshurst Park, and said to have been planted on the christening of Sir Philip Sidney in 1554, the Sidney Oak, or Bear Oak, is in fact much older – possibly 1,000 years – and had been growing for some 500 years when the Sidneys first came to Penshurst in 1552.

Sir Philip Sidney was a prominent figure in the Elizabethan age, famous as a poet, courtier and soldier. Remembered as the author of *Astrophil and Stella*, *The Defence of Poetry* (both 1581) and *The Countess of Pembroke's Arcadia* (1580), he wrote much of his work under the shade of the Sidney Oak.

The Sidney family secured the oak's legacy by planting acorns from the tree all over the world, as far afield as Sydney, Australia. In addition to this, saplings from genetic cloning are due to be planted on the estate, which, unlike the dying tree clinging to life after recently being set on fire by vandals, has changed little over the centuries.

That Taller tree, which of a nut was set
At his great birth,
*   where all the muses met*
There in the writhed Bark
*   are cut the names*
Of many Silvan, taken with the flames.

From *To Penhurst in The Forest*,
Ben Jonson (1572–1637)

Within the hollow of it there is a seat and it is capable of containing five or six persons with ease. The bark round the entrance is so much grown that it has recently been cut away to facilitate access.

***Country Gentleman's Magazine*,**
May 1794

ABOVE: The forlorn remains of the Oak in 2008.

LEFT: The Sidney Oak, c.1905.

St Dunstan's Oak
HEADCORN, KENT 42

Dunstan is the patron saint of goldsmiths. A blacksmith, jeweller and painter, he dedicated his life to God and eventually became Archbishop of Canterbury in 961. He crowned three Saxon kings and the service he devised remains the basis for contemporary British coronations.

He was famed for his confrontations with the devil, whose hoof he allegedly shod with a horseshoe. Dunstan removed it only after the devil promised never to enter a place where a horseshoe hung over the door – supposedly the origin of the lucky horseshoe. Born *c*.910, he died in 988 and was canonised in 1029.

The large Oak in the churchyard at St Peter and St Paul's in Headcorn was dedicated to him, and was in all probability standing tall in his lifetime. The huge hollow 9-m (29.5-ft) trunk caught fire on 25 April 1989 but continued to grow until 1993 when it finally gave up the ghost. The collapsed ivy-clad hulk sits in the shadow of two young trees that have been grown from its acorns.

ABOVE: St Dunstan's Oak in 1891.
ABOVE LEFT: The forlorn remains of the Oak in 2009.

St Dunstan, as the story goes,
Once pull'd the devil by the nose
With red-hot tongs,
*   which made him roar,*
That he was heard three miles or more.
English folk rhyme

The Old Oak Tree Restaurant

COBHAM, SURREY 43

This wonderful old oak at the aptly named Old Oak Tree Restaurant in Cobham was once a hub of activity, sitting on the corner of the Portsmouth Road and Copse Road. The Cobham Cycling Club had their headquarters there, and H. Baldock's Motor and Cycle Works were housed at the rear of the premises. The large girthed pollarded oak was accessible by stepladder and visitors could take tea within its boughs. Unfortunately, there is no sign of the tree today – it belongs to a time when Britain celebrated its eccentricities, of which this is certainly a great example. A sigh of relief then for health and safety.

BELOW: The Old Oak Tree Restaurant being put to good use in 1911.

The Crouch Oak

ADDLESTONE, SURREY 44 🍃

The Crouch Oak at Addlestone, which still stands majestically on Crouch Oak Lane, used to mark the boundary of Windsor Forest. Its name may be derived from its low crouching shape, from the prop that supports one of its main branches, or even from a marker cross that was once placed upon it.

It is another 'gospel tree' (see also the Battle Oak and the Wesley Tree) and was long known as Wycliffe's Oak, after John Wycliffe (1330–1384) who reportedly preached here after he was thrown out of Oxford for his evangelical views. The Baptist preacher Charles Spurgeon (1834–1892) delivered a sermon here in 1872 to a large crowd, continuing the Gospel Oak tradition.

Lieutenant Colonel de Visme, a local landowner, fenced off the area *c.*1810 in order to prevent the local maidens from stripping the tree's bark as they were using it to make their love potions!

The tree has hardly changed in over more than a century, apart from in 2001 the removal of a large upper branch, which was given to the local historical society. Tree-ring analysis by experts from University College London (UCL) dated the branch to 1670, and, with the hollow trunk measuring 7.3m (23.9ft), this lends credence to claims of the tree being up to 1,000 years old.

Disaster was narrowly avoided on Christmas night in 2007, thanks to the efforts of the local fire brigade, after vandals set fire to the tree by lighting paper placed in its hollow trunk.

CROUCH OAK, ADDLESTONE.

ABOVE: An engraving of the Crouch Oak, c.1850.

ABOVE: The tree in 2008.
LEFT: The Crouch Oak in 1903.

The Leith Hill Oak

DORKING, SURREY 45 🌿

Leith Hill near Dorking is the highest point in the southeast of England, rising to 294m (965ft) above sea level, and it is said that it affords magnificent views of 13 counties on a clear day.

With the assistance of a telescope Windsor Castle, Frant Church, St Paul's Cathedral, Dunstable Downs, Ditchling Beacon and the spires and towers of forty-one churches can be seen.

J S Bright, 1876

An old Oak once stood on the southeast face of Leith Hill, and it no doubt prospered for so long due in part to its sheltered position, which offered some protection from the elements. All the same, its large hollow trunk had clearly taken a battering over the years and it no longer remains.

Ethelwulf, father of Alfred the Great, helped secure the future of England by defeating the Danes here in 851 in a major battle that involved up to 40,000 men. 'Rivers of blood' were said to have flowed down the hillside.

The tower on the summit was built in 1766 by Richard Hull of Leith Hill Place (later the residence of the composer Ralph Vaughan Williams). It was erected for his own amusement and for 'the enjoyment of others'. When he died in 1772, he was buried upside-down beneath the tower. Believing that the world would turn on its axis before Judgement Day, he wished to stand before his maker 'the right way up'.

…the cattle, forsaking their pasture, are crowding for shelter beneath the spreading boughs of that mighty oak which stands like a thunder-blasted giant, riven and scarred by the fire of heaven, but still erect and defiant as ever.

From *The New York Times*, David Kep, 13 June 1886

ABOVE: Leith Hill Oak, c.1925.

The King's Oak
TILFORD, SURREY 46 🌿

Once regarded as 'the finest oak in Surrey', hollow and gnarled with a huge girth of 8.58m (28.15ft), the King's Oak is believed to be upwards of 800 years old. In 1952, it measured 8m (26ft) in girth, so it has grown by half a metre (1.6ft) in the last 50 years. William Cobbett (1763–1835), the celebrated journalist and writer, described his visit to the tree thus:

We veered a little to the left after we came to Tilford, at which place on the Green we stopped to look at an oak tree, which, when I was a little boy, was but a very little tree, comparatively, and which is now, take it altogether, by far the finest tree that I ever saw in my life. The stem or shaft is short; that is to say, it is short before you come to the first limbs; but it is full thirty feet round, at about eight or ten feet from the ground. Out of the stem there come not less than fifteen or sixteen limbs, many of which are from five to ten feet round, and each of which would, in fact, be considered a decent stick of timber. I am not judge enough of timber to say anything about the quantity in the whole tree, but my son stepped the ground, and, as nearly as we could judge, the diameter of the extent of the branches was upwards of ninety feet, which would make a circumference of about three hundred feet. The tree is in full growth at this moment. There is a little hole in one of the limbs; but with that exception, there appears not the smallest sign of decay.

Sadly, the same could hardly be said today, as this once grand Oak is a shadow of its former self. On a visit to the tree some 17 years ago I was mightily impressed, but a recent excursion left me reeling. Many of the major branches have been removed, and most worrying is the fact that the lower branches have gone. In their decaying years, ancient trees often shed their crowns, relying on their lower branches to survive. Hopefully, the King's Oak at Tilford will continue to manage that for many years to come. The King's Oak was formerly known as 'Novel's Oak' after the labourer who saved it in the story recounted below. This tale shows just how important ancient trees were to people long before conservation became a popular issue. The nearby public-house mentioned is the still-trading Barley Mow.

ABOVE: *Tilford Bridge and Oak* by Gordon Home, 1931.

ABOVE: The King's Oak at Tilford in 1906.

This Oak, which is said still to contain seventeen or eighteen loads of timber, stands upon the waste belonging to the see of Winchester, and, many years ago (in the time I believe of Bishop North), was marked to be felled. The workmen were about to commence, but their hearts failed at the thought of destroying so magnificent a tree; and one of them, by name Novel (a common name among the labourers hereabouts), proposed adjourning to a neighbouring public-house, to prepare their spirits for the execution, by sundry draughts of ale. These potations continued some time; and, while they were so engaged, a messenger arrived at full speed to reprieve the tree! Had not Novel's proposal been assented to, the bark would have been stripped round the trunk, and the tree irrecoverably ruined. From this circumstance, it has always, within my recollection, bourne the name of Novel's Oak; whence Manning and Bray derived their name of King's Oak, I know not.

From *The Gardener's Magazine and Register of Rural and Domestic Improvement*, H L Long, 1838

On the green between the two bridges at Telford, stands a venerable oak, of great size, but in full vigour, which is supposed to be the oak described in this charter, being at this day called the King's Oak.

From *History of Surrey (Volume III)*, Manning and Bray, 1814

LEFT: The King's Oak in 2008.

Queen Elizabeth's Oak

COWDRAY PARK, MIDHURST, WEST SUSSEX 47 ·

This wondrous old tree is officially the third largest sessile Oak in Great Britain. Measuring up at a whopping 12.67m (41.57ft) around the trunk, it is completely hollow with a large opening but remains in remarkably good health. Up to 1,000 years old, it is a very good example of how ancient trees shed their upper trunk and branches in their old age

ABOVE: Much reduced, cave-like and hollow – the Queen Elizabeth's Oak in 2009.

and rely on the lower branches for survival. The two photographs taken almost a century apart confirm the difference.

Queen Elizabeth I sheltered from a storm beneath its branches on a visit to the Cowdray Estate in 1591 and commented on the fine stature of the Oak. It was here that she rested her bow on the tree whilst hunting for deer. Cowdray Park hosts many other fine old trees, including some huge Sweet Chestnuts, but none match the splendour of this huge cavernous beast.

In the year 1591 he (Anthony Brone) was not too old to entertain Elizabeth and her Court for a week at Cowdray. Concerning this visit it is recorded that the Queen was "magnificently entertained", and her principal amusement seems to have been shooting deer in the Park. She killed three or four, and "Queen Elizabeth's Oak", against which she is said to have rested her bow, is still to be seen. Tradition has it that Lady Kildare (sister of Lord Montague) incurred the displeasure of the Queen by daring to shoot with her, and although she only killed one deer, we read Elizabeth was so annoyed "that she (Lady Kildare) did not afterwards dine at the royal table".

From *Cowdray: its Early History*, Torrens Trotter, 1932

RIGHT: The Queen Elizabeth's Oak, c.1921. Note the man blending in with the bark.

Queen Elizabeth's Oak

NORTHIAM, EAST SUSSEX 48 🍂

Whilst journeying to Rye on 11 August 1573, Queen Elizabeth I stopped for refreshment at Northiam. She was treated to a banquet under the shade of the great Oak on the village green, served up by George Bishop and his family from their home – the neighbouring Hayes Farm (now Hayes Inn).

She changed her shoes of 'green damask silk with heels of 2½ inches and pointed toes' and left them there as a memento for the villagers. They were given to a maid under the employ of the local and influential Frewen family, who claimed the shoes, and in whose possession they remain, passed down from father to son. Stored away safely in a bank vault, now they rarely see the light of day.

The current Lord Frewen gave them a special outing in 2010 to take the photograph shown here.

The Virgin Queen, apparently taken with the picnic, stopped there again three days later to eat a meal on her return journey. The Oak must have held a special place in Elizabeth's heart – this is the fourth named after

ABOVE: Queen Elizabeth's 'shoes of green damask silk', 2010.

her in this volume, and there are many more. These trees offered a place to sit and contemplate as well as providing shade to help maintain her ghostly pallor.

The tree is now dead, but the large ivy-clad stump remains rooted to the ground with a girth of 7.35m (24.11ft), a young tree growing beside it having supposedly taken from its roots. I would guess that it is upwards of 700 years old, having been a mature tree at the time of its most famous visitor over 435 years ago. Also in the churchyard stands a fragmented 1,000-year-old Yew with a 6.38m (20.9ft) girth.

ABOVE: Queen Elizabeth's Oak, c.1915.

ABOVE: Queen Elizabeth's Oak, c.1910.

ABOVE: Queen Elizabeth Oak's stump in 2010.

The New Forest

HAMPSHIRE

Although not so ancient as some of our forests in Britain, the New Forest can hardly be described as 'new', the area being well known in Saxon times. It was created in 1079, primarily as a deer hunting ground, by William the Conqueror, who set up specific laws to protect it (many of which are still in place today) and which were upheld by the local verderers (forest judicial officers).

The forest hosts many fine trees and is still grazed by the famous New Forest ponies, sheep and cattle. The ancient commoners' right to 'pannage' is retained for 60 days in the autumn, when pigs are allowed under the trees to eat the acorns and beech nuts, which are poisonous to the ponies. In 1999, the New Forest was designated a National Park, preserving the 141-acre site for the general public.

Charcoal burning was one of the New Forest's earliest industries, although it is a rarer occurrence today. The charcoal produced had a multitude of uses, particularly in the smelting of iron. However, Queen Elizabeth I became so concerned at the loss of trees when England needed timber for building ships that she passed a law preventing the felling of trees for charcoal production.

The Cadenham Oak, about three miles from Lyndhurst, is another of the remarkable trees of the New Forest. This tree, which buds every year at Christmas, is mentioned by Camden. "Having heard of this oak," says Gilpin, "I took to see it on the 29th December, 1781. Having had the account of its early budding confirmed on the spot, I engaged one Michael Lawrence, who kept the White Hart, a small alehouse in the neighbourhood, to send me some of the leaves as soon as they should appear. The man, who had not the least doubt about the matter, kept his word, and sent me several twigs on the 5th of January, 1782. The leaves were fairly expanded, about 1 inch in length.

From *The Trees and Shrubs of Britain*, John Loudon, 1838

ABOVE: The Rufus Stone c1910.

The Rufus Stone

NEW FOREST, HAMPSHIRE

An inscription on the stone reads:
Here stood the oak tree on which an arrow shot by Sir Walter Tyrrell at a stag glanced and struck King William the Second surnamed Rufus on the breast of which he instantly died on the second day of August Anno 1100.

William Rufus's brother Richard also met his death in the New Forest by 'a pestilential blast', while the king's nephew – another Richard – died either by being shot by an arrow or strangulation after being caught in the boughs of a tree in the forest. Whether this was an uncanny trio of coincidences or a medieval trio of assassinations is open to speculation.

ABOVE: Woodcutters engraving, c.1850.

The Knightwood Oak

The Knightwood Oak is not only the New Forest's most famous tree but also, at around 600 years old, probably its oldest. The girth of the trunk is 7.38m (24.21ft), making it the largest Oak in the forest.

Like many other ancient trees, the Knightwood Oak has been pollarded. This is the practice whereby a tree is cut a couple of metres above the ground in order to promote a dense growth of fresh branches, out of the reach of any grazing animals. These new shoots were harvested during the autumn every seven to fifteen years and were then used for poles, firewood and fencing. Practised throughout Britain from ancient times, the pollarding of Oak trees was stopped during the eighteenth century when the Royal Navy needed the timber to build ships for Nelson's fleet at Bucklers Hard, Hampshire.

Pollarding prohibited the growth of tall, solid trunks, which were required for cutting planks. The practice, which has been out of use for some 200 years, is now being revived in the New Forest and elsewhere across Britain.

ABOVE: The Knightwood Oak in 1925.

ABOVE The Knightwood Oak, c.1905.

ABOVE: The tree in 2008.

The King and Queen Oaks

BOLDERWOOD, NEW FOREST, HAMPSHIRE 50

The Oaks here do not grow so high or so large as in many other parts of England, but they are far finer in their outlines, hanging in the distance as if rather suspended in the air than growing from the earth, but nearer, as especially at Bramble Hill, twisting their long arms, and interlacing each other into a thick roof. Now and then they take to straggling ways, running out, as with the famous Knightwood Oak, into mere awkward forks. The most striking are not, perhaps, so much those in their prime, as the old ruined trees at Bolderwood, their bark furrowed with age, their timber quite decayed, now only braced together by the clamps of ivy to which they once gave support and strength.

John Richard de Capel Wise

The Bolderwood area of the New Forest hosts many fine old Oaks and was reputed to be Queen Victoria's favourite part of the forest when she visited. Secluded from the main tracks and inaccessible by car, it has managed to preserve some of the oldest trees.

ABOVE: The King and Queen Oaks, Bolderwood, New Forest c. 1905.

ABOVE: Another old Oak at Black Knole, New Forest in 2008.

ABOVE: An old Oak at Queens Bower, Bolderwood, New Forest, c. 1915.

The Eagle Oak

NEW FOREST, HAMPSHIRE 51 🍃

The story of the Eagle Oak is a sad one. Standing not far from the Knightwood Oak, with a girth of 5.4m (17.7ft) and probably the second oldest Oak in the forest, it was a resting place for the last English sea eagle (also known as the white-tailed eagle), which was shot from its branches by a New Forest ranger in 1810. But 200 years later, plans are underfoot to reintroduce the bird to East Anglia, so we may yet again see its graceful presence.

BELOW: The Eagle Oak, alive and well if a little suffocated by conifers in 2010.

Savernake Forest
WILTSHIRE

Savernake Forest is absolutely packed with remarkable ancient trees, and one grotesque, twisted, living statue follows another. Standing just south of Marlborough, and a surviving remnant of Wiltshire's ancient 'Royal Forests', it is referred to as 'Safernoc' in a Saxon charter of King Athelstan in AD934. Given by William the Conqueror as a reward to a victorious Norman knight for his part in the Battle of Hastings in 1066, the forest has remained in family hands ever since, for 31 generations, and is the only ancient British forest not owned by the Crown.

In Tudor times, the family head was Sir John Seymour, the father of Jane, the girl who caught the eye of Henry VIII when he was on a deer hunting trip whilst married to Anne Boleyn. Henry and Jane were married just 11 days after Queen Anne was beheaded for adultery in 1536. Queen Jane managed to keep her head, but she died a few days after childbirth, having borne the king his only son.

In the mid-eighteenth century, the forest covered some 40,000 acres, almost ten times its current size. Around this time, the then owner, Lord Thomas Bruce, commissioned Lancelot 'Capability' Brown to plant great Beech avenues, including the 'Grand Avenue', which, running straight at 6.3km (3.9 miles) long, is the longest Beech avenue in Britain.

By the mid-nineteenth century, the estate was continuing to manage a huge deer park, and tolls were charged at the gates where the current A4 road passes through the forest. These days, access to the forest is free to the public.

Surviving the timber demands of the Second World War and its use as an ammunition dump, Savernake has since been managed by the Forestry Commission. Now designated a Site of Special Scientific Interest (SSSI), the ancient trees have been given a new lease of life through a forest-wide project of scrub clearance and the re-opening of historic avenues.

RIGHT: Savernake Forest 'Homeward Bound', c.1925.

ABOVE: A huge Oak in Savernake Forest, surrounded by its own fallen limbs in 2008.

The Big Belly Oak

SAVERNAKE FOREST, WILTSHIRE 52 🍃

*Dance naked round the Big Belly Oak 12 times anti-clockwise
and you shall summon the devil.*

ABOVE: Swallowed whole by the Big Belly Oak in 2008.

ABOVE LEFT: The Big Belly Oak, Savernake Forest, c.1925.

Rooted precariously at the side of the busy A346 road, the aptly named Big Belly Oak, also known as 'The Decanter Oak' owing to its bulbous hollow trunk, is one of Savernake's oldest and most famous trees. Thought to be between 1,000 and 1,100 years old, it could have taken root at around the time of Alfred the Great. Henry VIII might well have ridden past the tree whilst hunting for deer in the forest, as he is said to have met Jane Seymour, his third wife, in the area. At 500–600 years old, the tree would have been an impressive size in his time.

It now measures 11.15m (36.58ft) in girth and, in spite of losing most of its crown, still maintains a healthy growth each summer. In 2002, it was braced by the Forestry Commission to try and stem a huge crack that threatened to split the tree in half.

You could try the devil's dance (see above), but the treacherous A346 may have the better of you.

The King Oak
SAVERNAKE FOREST, WILTSHIRE 53

The King Oak in Savernake Forest – a tree which carries back the imagination not only to the days when Norman hunters came to rest under its spreading branches, but to the earlier times when, in this sylvan temple, with massive trunks for its pillars, and solemn shade for its canopy, the venerable tree looked down on heathen rites.

William Sydney Gibson, 1858

ABOVE: The replacement King Oak. The King is dead, long live the King!

BELOW: The King Oak, Savernake Forest, 1901.

The Braydon Oak

SAVERNAKE FOREST, WILTSHIRE 54 ◖

Of all the trees that I have hunted whilst researching for this book, the Braydon Oak was the most elusive. It sits in long grass way off the beaten track, but it was not always so. A century ago, afternoon teas were sold at nearby Braydonhook Lodge to visitors, but now the lodge is overgrown and has fallen into disrepair, although there are plans to renovate it.

The tree has a large girth of 7.10m (23.29ft) and is remarkable for its age insofar as it still stands incredibly tall, although it has lost a large branch, which lies beside it, measuring 3.7m (12.1ft) in circumference, itself the size of a mature tree.

LEFT: The Braydon Oak in 2009.

BELOW: The Braydon Oak, Savernake Forest, 1906.

Gog and Magog
GLASTONBURY, SOMERSET 55

These two giant trees are all that remain of a once magnificent avenue of Oaks that led across Stonedown towards Glastonbury Tor, a mile to the southeast, supposedly planted 2,000 years ago by the Druids.

Also known as 'The Avalon Oaks', many were felled around 1906 to enlarge a farm and were sold to the local timber merchants J Snow & Son. The diameter of one of the trees measured 3.35m (10.9ft), equating roughly to a circumference of 10.5m (34.4ft), lending little credit to the 2,000 annual growth rings that were counted at the time. I wonder if both dark and light rings were counted (each representing spring and summer growth) as Oaks rarely live much beyond 1,200 years. This would bring the age of the tree to a more conceivable 1,000 years. If the avenue was planted by the Druids, it makes sense that any new trees would have been sown from local acorns as the older trees died, thus continuing the tradition. This would make Magog, at 7.5m (24.6ft) in girth, a rare living sentinel to Britain's ancient inhabitants, as Gog now stands dead with a waist of 7.3m (23.9ft).

The Glastonbury Conservation Society has planted some new Oaks commemorating the ancient Druidic grove.

Goemagot, in stature twelve cubits, and of such prodigious strength that at one shake he pulled up an oak as if it had been a hazel wand.

From *History of the Kings of Britain*, Geoffrey of Monmouth, *c.*1136

OPPOSITE: Gog and Magog in 2009.
BELOW: Tree felling in Glastonbury, *c.*1930.

The Legend of Gog and Magog

The Roman Emperor Diocletian had 33 wayward daughters. To calm their ways he found them husbands whom the sisters, led by the eldest Alba, conspired to murder by slitting their throats as they lay sleeping. Cast adrift on a ship, they came to Britain (then known as Albion), where they paired with demons, creating a race of giants from their unnatural offspring.

Brutus led his defeated refugee army here from Troy, renaming Albion after himself as 'Britain'. All the giants were slain, with the exception of their leader Goemagot (Gogmagog), whom Brutus's champion Corineus killed in single combat by hurling him from a high rock into the sea to his death.

A variant on the story tells how Brutus brought the last two giants Gog and Magog to his palace in London. Here they were chained as protectors of the palace, where they remain as effigies to this day at the same spot, the site of the current Guildhall.

Gog and Magog appear as different characters in the Bible and the Koran, as harbingers of death and destruction and enemies of religion. Twin hills in Cambridgeshire are named after them, and giant figures of them were carved into the slope on the approach to Plymouth Hoe. A pair of trees that was named after them is mentioned in Strutt's *Sylva Brittanica*.

That they have survived in one form or another illustrates the power that they once held over people. In Britain, Gog is probably a corruption of the Celtic god Ogmios, and Magog his female counterpart. The original wicker effigies of the pair at the Guildhall were destroyed during the Blitz in 1940 and were replaced with wooden statues in 1953. New wicker figures made in 2006 are paraded at the Lord Mayor's show as they have been since the reign of Henry V, echoing ancient pagan sacrificial ceremonies. The fear that they invoked points to them being the pagan deities to which poor martyrs were sacrificed.

It adds kudos to the trees at Glastonbury that they were planted by Druid priests. People still leave offerings to this day.

RIGHT: Gog.
FAR RIGHT: Magog.

LEFT AND ABOVE: Gog and Magog at the Guildhall, London.
BELOW: An offering to the pair.

Cromwell's Oak

MELKSHAM, WILTSHIRE 56 🌰

Cromwell's Oak, or the Gibbet Oak as it is also known, stands in a field not far from the Wiltshire market town of Melksham. It was so named after Oliver Cromwell under whose orders four men were hanged from the tree for pillaging in 1643. They were almost certainly Royalist soldiers taken prisoner at a nearby battle, the hanging being commensurate with Cromwell's tyrannical nature.

The tree itself would certainly have been fit for purpose, standing, as it does, with a large hollow waistline of 6.68m (21.9ft) at 1m (3.28ft) from the ground, and it is believed to be 700 years old. Its inner wall is blackened from fire, raising concerns over its future survival, but Melksham Oak Community School, which opened in 2010, has in effect become its new 'Lord Protector'.

ABOVE: Cromwell's Oak in 1905.

LEFT: Cromwell's Oak in 2009, with the school construction visible beyond.

Twin Turkeys

ABOVE LEFT: A Turkey Oak dwarfs the author, 2008.

ABOVE: A Turkey Oak in 2008.

These two great Turkey Oaks were planted *c.*1720 by the Penruddocke family around the time that the species was first introduced to Britain. They differ from our English Oaks in that they grow much faster – this pair both measured 8m (26.2ft) in girth – a feat that would take our native Oak trees far longer than 300 years to achieve.

Found around the Mediterranean in the region from France to Turkey, these trees were extensively planted in Britain in the sixteenth century, but the timber was found to be of inferior quality to that of the English Oak. The species has recently fallen out of favour due to it hosting the knopper gall wasp, which destroys the acorns of our native Oaks. Eradication of the tree is planned in the New Forest for this very reason.

These two fine trees, meanwhile, remain the joint contenders as county champions of the species in Wiltshire.

Wyndham's Oak

SILTON, DORSET 58 ·

ABOVE: Tea party at Wyndham's Oak in 2009.

ABOVE: Wyndham's Oak, c. 1945.

ABOVE: The hollow trunk of Wyndham's Oak in 2009.

Wyndham's Oak is thought to be 1,000 years old and, at 9.79m (32.12ft), possesses the largest girth of any tree in Dorset. Also known as the 'Judge's Tree', it was named after Judge Hugh Wyndham who purchased an estate at Silton in 1641. He was the Justice of the Common Pleas in the time of Charles II and used to sit within the tree and smoke his pipe to relax and contemplate. A life-size statue of him dominates the parish church, just as he no doubt once dominated the parish.

Reports of hangings from the tree after the Monmouth Rebellion of 1685 probably point to the activities of local rebels from nearby villages. The large branch visible in the painting (opposite) was high enough in the late-nineteenth century for a cart to be ridden beneath it, but by the time of the photograph (above right) it was close to the ground. In 1948, it came down, leaving the tree with the rounded shape we see today. The current owner of the farm remembers losing a cow, only to find it two days later stuck firmly inside the hollow trunk.

In point of form and picturesque effect it yields to none; its hollowed trunk, having scarce any intestinal life; its head bald, yet majestic in decay, and many of its lateral limbs withered, presenting a fine contrast to the few vigorous survivors.

From *Antiquarian and Topographical Cabinet*, James Sargant Storer and John Greig, 1810

ABOVE: *Wyndham's Oak* painted by J G Surgey (1851 – 1883).

The Meavy Oak
MEAVY, DEVON 59

At the southwestern reaches of Dartmoor, on a picturesque village green, stands the old Meavy Oak. During my visit, a heavy mist descended on the moor and I was met by a sustained choir of voices emanating from the neighbouring Royal Oak pub. The singers were a visiting group of bellringers from Wadebridge in Cornwall, who, after peeling at St Peter's church, had stopped for some prolonged refreshment. The whole scene transported me back to a bygone age.

The Oak itself is believed to have been planted in the reign of King John, some 900 years ago, and was used as a Gospel Oak or open-air pulpit before the church was built in the early thirteenth century. It stands at 6.56m (21.52ft) in girth beside the Meavy Cross, which it pre-dates by 400 years, outside the church gate. The now hollow trunk was probably much larger once but it still produces a good crown with a fine crop of acorns.

Every year on the third Saturday of June, the village still hosts the Meavy Oak fair, which includes a demonstration of maypole dancing by local schoolchildren, a practice that the Meavy Oak may have witnessed for almost a millennium.

The Meavy Oak is referred to in deeds almost to the Conquest, and that it was a sacred tree to which certain amount of reverence was given is probable enough. The cross was set up under its shadow to consecrate it and probably put an end to superstitious rites done there. Anyhow this tree till within this century was, on the village festival, surrounded with poles, a platform was erected above the tree, the top of which was kept clipped flat like a table, and a set of stairs erected, by means of which the platform could be reached. On the top a table and chairs were set and feasting took place. Whether dancing I cannot say, but in all probability in former generations there was dancing there as well as feeding and drinking. These trees where dancing took place are precisely the Maypole in a primitive form.

From *A Book of the West, Volume I, Devon,* Reverend Sabine Baring-Gould, 1900

RIGHT: The Meavy Oak in 2009.

The Last Oak in England

PENZANCE, CORNWALL 60

Fittingly, the last tree featured in this chapter is 'The Last Oak in England', on the road from Penzance to Land's End. According to Arthurian legend, the ancient land of Lyonesse once joined Land's End to the Scilly Isles, and it was home to Tristan, one of King Arthur's knights, until a great deluge some 1,500 years ago flooded the land, where it remains submerged to this day. Lord Tennyson named it as the site of Arthur's final battle, where he was mortally wounded by Mordred.

Apparently, if you look hard enough, the petrified sunken trunks of great Oaks can still be seen beneath the water.

Then rose the King and moved his host by night
And ever pushed Sir Mordred, league by league,
Back to the sunset bound of Lyonesse –
A land of old upheaven from the abyss
By fire, to sink into the abyss again;
Where fragments of forgotten peoples dwelt,
And the long mountains ended in a coast
Of ever-shifting sand, and far away
The phantom circle of a moaning sea.

From *Idylls of the King*, Alfred, Lord Tennyson
(published between 1856 and 1885)

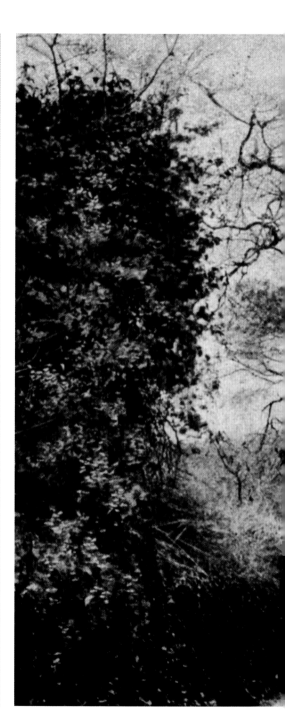

RIGHT: The Last Oak in England, Penzance, 1906.

CHAPTER TWO

The Elm

English Elm *(Ulmus procera)*
Wych Elm *(Ulmus glabra)*

COME, I WILL FASTEN ON THIS SLEEVE OF THINE;
THOU ART AN ELM, MY HUSBAND, I A VINE;
WHOSE WEAKNESS, MARRIED TO THY STRONGER STATE,
MAKES ME WITH THY STRENGTH TO COMMUNICATE.
WILLIAM SHAKESPEARE *COMEDY OF ERRORS* (c.1589–1594)

ABOVE: Elm flower.
OPPOSITE: Dinton Elm in seed.

The tall, abounding elm, that grows,
  In hedgerows up and down;
In field and forest, copse and park,
  And in the peopled town;
With colonies of noisy rooks,
  That nestle in its crown.

Thomas Hood (1789–1845)

Principally Britain hosts three main varieties of Elm – the English Elm, which is more common in the Midlands and southern England, the Wych Elm, a more hardy species which is better suited to grow in the north and by the sea, and the Smooth-leaved Elm.

There was a time not too long ago when the Elm rivalled the Oak as our most common broad-leaved tree, but that was before the onslaught of the dreaded Dutch Elm Disease, which devastated our native Elm population to such an extent in the late 1970s that these beautiful trees are now very rare. Indeed, almost all of the ancient Elms that are featured in the following pages are now long gone. There are exceptions, however, and Brighton, in particular, has become the Elm capital of Britain. East Anglia and pockets of Scotland and Wales also host some fine trees. Some young Elms still survive in our hedgerows, as the beetle that carries the disease prefers the thick, roughened bark of mature trees.

Growing to a height of 30m (98.4ft), the branches can spread out 12m (39.3ft) from the trunk, which, after a century, tends to hollow. The timber is tough and particularly suited for use in wet conditions, where it can last for centuries without rotting. The Elm is shallow rooted and known for suddenly falling, as are its branches, onto whoever may be sitting below at the time – an ill-advised occupation.

Maude's Elm

CHELTENHAM, GLOUCESTERSHIRE 61

The story of Maude's Elm must go down as the most tragic tale in this book, to rival even those most famous tragedies of Greece, yet events such as these were not uncommon in medieval times.

Maude Bowen lived in the village of Swindon near Cheltenham with her mother, and they both worked as spinners. One day Maude took her wares to market in Cheltenham but never made it home again. She had previously declined the affections of both her uncle Godfrey Bowen and the Lord of Swindon Manor, who both conspired to have their way with her. Maude's lover, Walter Gray, heard of the conspiracy and travelled to Cheltenham to save her, but he arrived too late and discovered the avaricious uncle committing a sinful act with Maude. Unseen, he fired an arrow into Godfrey's heart, killing him, and then fled, as did the Lord, but Maude lay dead, drowned face-down in the river.

It was decreed by the Lord of the Manor that Maude must have committed suicide and, in keeping with the customs of the time, she was buried at the nearest crossroads with a live elm stake through her heart to prevent her returning as a vampire. The stake took root and Maude's Elm is supposed to have grown from this into a fine tree that reached 6.4m (20.9ft) in girth, and 24.3m (79.7ft) in height.

Her mother was thrown out of her home and spent most of her remaining days mourning at her daughter's grave. One morning, as he travelled to Cheltenham, The Lord of Swindon Manor was annoyed to find her crying at the graveside and ordered his men to move her. She held fast and, as the men proceeded to remove her, one of them was shot dead by an arrow. Nobody saw that it was Walter, protecting his lover's mother, and she was found guilty of witchcraft and was sentenced to be burnt at Maude's Elm. During the ordeal, the bitter Lord taunted and mocked her, but another arrow from Walter's bow struck him dead and he fell into the flames alongside her.

The tree survived until 1907 when it was struck by lightning, deemed unsafe and felled, but the crossroads are still there, hiding the grisly remains of the 15-year-old beauty, Maude Bowen.

ABOVE: Maude's Elm, Cheltenham, c.1900.

O the old Elm Tree that for ages past,
Has Bowed its majestic head.
To the gentle breeze and the sturdy blast,
Still Flourished o'er the dead;
And whenever I gaze on its aspect bold,
Or give ear to its mournful creek,
Do I think what a tale would it unfold.
Could its leaves on its branches speak.

Traditional rhyme

120

The Ramsbury Elm

RAMSBURY, WILTSHIRE 62

The names of the Confederates against Her Majesty who have diverse and sundry times conspired her life and do daily confederate against her. Among others – Ould Birtles the great devel, Darnally the sorcerer, Maude Twogood enchantresse, the oulde witche of Ramsbury, several other old witches.

Calendar of State Papers, Domestic Series, of the reign of Elizabeth I, 1581–1590

As we enter (Ramsbury) we see the immemorial elm in the little square, a giant fellow, over twenty feet in circumference, shelter for men and birds, and a grand chattering place for both.

From *And So to Bath*, Cecil Roberts, 1940

An ancient Wych Elm dominated the village square at Ramsbury for at least 300 years, standing as it did in front of the Bell Inn, a coaching house on the Bath to London road. Local legend has it that in the sixteenth century a witch was buried among the roots of the tree and invoked a curse should the tree ever be removed.

By 1980, the tree had died from either Dutch Elm Disease or old age, and only a rotten stump remained. Consultation followed, and a village referendum narrowly voted by 356 to 339 votes to remove it, amongst allegations of foul play. In October 1986, with considerable village participation, a replacement Oak tree, which was sponsored by the Ramsbury Building Society (which adopted the Elm as its logo) and was brought in from Epping Forest, was planted in its place amidst festivities with the local schoolchildren dressing up as witches and scarecrows. There followed a storm, which wreaked havoc upon the town, and the celebrations had to continue indoors. However, if this was retribution from the old witch she certainly meant the new tree no harm as it still thrives today.

Ironically, the building society ceased trading at its Ramsbury headquarters that very same year – its demise coinciding with that of its emblem.

BELOW: The Old Elm at Ramsbury, c. 1912.

Latimer's Elm

HADLEY, HERTFORDSHIRE 63

Latimer's Elm is commonly thought to have been named after Hugh Latimer, the sixteenth-century Bishop of Worcester, who allegedly preached to Henry VIII under its branches. Latimer was burned at the stake outside Balliol College, Oxford, for clinging to his protestant beliefs, which, of course, made him a martyr. However, the tree could well have been named after a local man.

It measured over 6m (19.6ft) in girth in 1876, and was cut down in 1935, some fifteen years after the photograph (right) was taken.

Sometimes confused with the Elm is 'The Warwick Oak' (below), whose rotting stump was removed in the Second World War. It is reputed to be the spot where Richard Neville, 16th Earl of Warwick, was killed. He had led the Lancastrian army against the Yorkists at the Battle of Barnet in 1471 – the decisive battle of the War of the Roses – but, in the face of defeat, he was struck down whilst trying to escape the battlefield.

ABOVE: Latimer's Elm, c. 1920.
BELOW: The Warwick Oak, c. 1905.

Hunter's Elm

BRENTWOOD, ESSEX 64

When Mary I ascended the throne in 1553, she ushered in the restoration of the Roman Catholic Church in England. With it came the persecution of almost 300 dissenters, who were burned at the stake, earning her the title of 'Bloody Mary'.

One such 'Marian Martyr' was William Hunter, who, aged 19, and found reading his Bible in Brentwood chapel was accused of heresy and taken to the local justice William Browne and thence to Bishop Bonner in London, and both times refused to accept the Catholic dogma of transubstantiation – the belief that bread and wine changed into the body and blood of Jesus Christ. The bishop even offered him £40 and the chance to become a 'Freeman of the City' if he would repent, but he stuck to his guns and was returned to Brentwood where he was duly burned at the stake on 27 March 1555.

Hunter's Elm was planted on the spot where he met his fate to commemorate the martyr and was measured at 8.2m (26.9ft) in girth 1m (3.281ft) from the ground in 1852. By 1870, the tree looked quite dead, and by 1900, when the photograph was taken, it appeared to have been more brick than tree. Deemed unsafe, the decayed remains of the stump were finally removed in 1952, but not before an Oak was planted in recognition of the martyr and to celebrate the assession of George VI in 1936.

RIGHT: Hunter's Elm, c. 1900.

123

The Old Elm
HAVERING-ATTE-BOWER, GREATER LONDON 65

ABOVE LEFT: Havering Elm, stock and whipping post, c.1920.

ABOVE: *The Stocks, Havering-Atte-Bower* by Burliegh Bruhl, watercolour, 1909.

Havering-atte-Bower is perched on one of the highest points in London and it is steeped in history. King Edward the Confessor built a hunting lodge here, which became a palace, or 'bower'. There is evidence to suggest that he may have died here in 1066, and there is no doubt at all that Joan of Navarre, second queen to Henry IV, did die here in 1437.

The Elm on the green would have been over 100 years old by then, so we see illustrated a 700-year-old tree. Much later, the hollow trunk was bricked up in an effort to hold it together. In 1955, the top was lost in a gale and, despite local protests, it was burned out as part of a controlled removal by Romford Council in 1956.

In 1966 and again in 2009, the stocks and whipping post were restored and are protected by a preservation order. They replaced originals dating to 1829, but stocks have stood on the green since the seventeenth century in order to 'punish and secure offenders'.

Byron's Elm

There is a spot in the churchyard, near the footpath, on the brow of a hill looking towards Windsor, and a tomb under a large tree (bearing the name of Peachie, or Peachey), where I used to sit for hours and hours when a boy: this was my favourite spot…

Lord Byron, writing a letter to John Murray on the death of his daughter Allegra, 26 May 1822

Lord Byron declared the Peachey tomb in St Mary's churchyard his 'favourite spot'. It sat under a great Elm tree, which became known as Byron's Elm and, by the time of this photograph (below right), had been severely damaged by lightning. It was here that the poet sat and wrote the lines shown (right) in 1807, which were set on a slab next to the tomb by Sir George Sinclair, the son of his schoolfriend, in 1905. In 1822, Byron's daughter Allegra was buried here when she died, aged only five years old.

Spot of my youth! whose hoary branches sigh,
Swept by the breeze that fans thy cloudless sky;
Where now alone I muse, who oft have trod,
With those I loved, thy soft and verdant sod;
With those who, scatter'd far,
*   perchance deplore,*
Like me, the happy scenes they knew before:
Oh! as I trace again thy winding hill,
Mine eyes admire, my heart adores thee still,
Thou drooping Elm!
*   beneath whose boughs I lay,*
And frequent mus'd the twilight hours away;
Where, as they once were wont,
*   my limbs recline,*
But, ah! without the thoughts which then
*   were mine:*
How do thy branches, moaning to the blast,
Invite the bosom to recall the past,
And seem to whisper, as they gently swell,
'Take, while thou canst, a lingering,
*   last farewell!'*

From *Lines Written Beneath an Elm in the Churchyard of Harrow*, George Gordon, Lord Byron, 1807

LEFT: Harrow-on-the-Hill from the Peachey Tomb.

BELOW: Byron's Elm and the Peachey Tomb, 1905.

The Lungs of London

HYDE PARK, LONDON 67

The Crystal Palace was erected to house the Great Exhibition of 1851. The project owed much to Henry Cole from the Royal Society who wanted to promote an 'exhibition of competition and encouragement' in art and industry. Backed by Prince Albert, he set out to better the grand exhibitions of France but could find nowhere to host the spectacle.

A competition was held to design a suitable building and 233 proposals were submitted. It was finally won by Joseph Paxton, who was later awarded a knighthood for his efforts. The Duke of Wellington suggested Hyde Park as the venue, but a public outcry followed when it was realised that three 27.4-m (90-ft) tall Elm trees would be lost in the process. After consultation, Paxton revised his plans by including a 32.9-m (108-ft) high arched transept to enclose the trees within the building, thereby transforming the original flat-roofed design. The largest of these Elm trees became known as 'The Lungs of London' and must have looked magnificent inside the huge structure. In contrast, there are no large Elms left standing in Hyde Park today since the onslaught of Dutch Elm Disease.

The Crystal Palace covered 198 acres, was built of iron and glass with wooden planking to walk on, and was completed on time. The exhibition was opened by Queen Victoria on 1 May 1851 and it was visited by six million people. The structure was dismantled and rebuilt at Sydenham the following year and remained there until 1936 when it was utterly destroyed by fire. The area around Sydenham has since became known as Crystal Palace.

Steel and Gold, and Coal and Wine,
Fabric Rough or Fairy-Fine
And shapes and hues of Art divine
All of beauty, All of Use
That one fair planet can produce.

Alfred, Lord Tennyson, on the Crystal Palace

ABOVE: The Crystal Palace and the Fountains at Sydenham, c.1861.

Dear Concerned Citizen of London,

I know that there have been many complaints and worries about the new Crystal Palace. Let me assure you, however, that all your worries have been taken care of. First of all, the elm trees standing in Rotten Row will not be destroyed or bothered in any way. The design of the palace has been altered so that a magnificent arched transept now covers the trees. The transept will do nothing to the structure of the building except preserve the trees and add magnificence to the palace.

If we can make a few small sacrifices now, we will gain much larger things in the long run for our country. We must all cooperate, and if everything goes smoothly, The Great Exhibition of the Industry of all Nations should open on May 1, 1851; right on schedule.

Sincerely,
Joseph Paxton

Letter from Joseph Paxton to reassure concerned citizens about the future of the Hyde Park Elms

LEFT: The last promenade at The Crystal Palace around 'The Lungs of London', from *The Illustrated London News*, 1 May 1852.

127

The Old Elm
YATTENDON, BERKSHIRE 68

This great hollow Elm dominated the square in the Berkshire village of Yattendon until 1973 when, like so many of its kind, it succumbed to the deadly Dutch Elm Disease. It was often mistaken as an Oak tree, due probably to the location of the Royal Oak pub beside it, where Oliver Cromwell dined the night before the Battle of Newbury in 1644. The tree could well have been there at that time. The Elm has now been replaced with an Oak, with seating added, similar to the Elm seen here.

ABOVE: The Old Elm at Yattendon, 1904.

The Centre Elm

BINFIELD, BERKSHIRE 69

The 800-year-old Centre Elm at Binfield once marked the centre of Windsor Forest, a sign of just how large the forest once was as Binfield is now miles away from its remnants. Most of the surrounding forest was cleared following the Enclosure Act of 1813, allowing people to buy the land for agriculture.

The tree was ravaged by Dutch Elm Disease in the 1970s, but the huge hollow trunk remained as a landmark – I remember being impressed by it when visiting Binfield in the late 1980s – so when I returned to photograph it I was surprised to discover that it had been removed in 2003 and not a trace survives.

The historic Stag and Hounds still stands, however, and it was previously used by Henry VIII and Elizabeth I as a royal hunting lodge. Queen Bess is reputed to have watched maypole dancing on the green outside. Cromwell's soldiers used it as a refuge during the Civil War, and the outlaw Dick Turpin may even have visited it during the eighteenth century, as it became a coaching inn in 1727.

The celebrated poet Alexander Pope lived at Binfield in the early eighteenth century, and a large Beech tree where he sat to write was named after him. William Cobbett, who made a series of journeys on horseback across southern England and recorded them in his *Rural Rides*, also stayed there and commented that it was 'a very nice place'. However, he was less complimentary about the neighbouring town of Bracknell, branding it a 'bleak and desolate place', and this, of course, was 140 years before its later mass development in the 1970s.

ABOVE: In 2008 with the new Oak tree replacement.

BELOW: The Centre Elm and the Stag and Hounds Inn at Binfield, 1892.

Queen Mary's Bower
HAMPTON COURT, SURREY 70

Queen Mary's Bower was planted on the West Terrace of The Privy Garden at Hampton Court in 1689, the year of Queen Mary's joint coronation with William III. It was so named because she used to walk within its shade. At that time, ladies would always keep out of the sun in order to maintain their ghostly white pallor – in contrast to today's tastes, a tan was considered vulgar in the seventeenth century and was sported only by labourers and peasants. The Wych Elm bower was 3.6m (11.8ft) wide and 90m (295ft) long, and Queen Mary purportedly spent a great deal of time there.

After visiting Hampton Court, the writer and gardener John Evelyn described the avenue in an entry in his diary on 2 June 1662:

The cradle-work of horne-beam in the garden is, for the perplexed twining of the trees, very observable.

This suggests that there was a previous avenue in the garden, which Mary's Bower replaced – a trend of replanting that would continue up to the present day. Uprooted in the 1690s, and then again in the 1720s, the bower eventually fell victim to Dutch Elm Disease in the 1970s. It was not until 1995, after extensive archaeological and historical research, that the gardens were laid out as Mary and William's gardens of 1690 would have looked. The bower was replanted with Hornbeam, which survives today, remaining useful for those visitors wanting to avoid the sun.

RIGHT: Queen Mary's Bower, c.1900.

The Elm Avenue

FARNHAM PARK, SURREY 71

There has been a castle at Farnham since 1138. Built by Henry de Blois, grandson of William the Conqueror, it became the seat of power for the Bishops of Winchester for over 800 years.

An avenue of Elms was planted by Bishop Morley around 1660 following the restoration of the monarchy – the castle and park had been laid to ruin after the Civil War in 1648. The trees ran for a kilometre along a mound at the highest part of Farnham Park for its entire length towards Farnham Castle. Gold coins dating from 52BC, which were found here, date the original old road to the Iron Age. Morley also set about the task of restoring the castle and grounds to their former glory.

Unfortunately, Dutch Elm Disease took hold in the 1970s and signalled the death knell for all of the 300-year-old Elms, but an avenue of Lime and Beech trees was planted in their place.

The park is lovely and full of splendid old trees. There is an avenue of elms three-quarters of a mile long, ending in two remarkably large trees, the bole of one being nineteen feet round, a yard from the ground, and the other eighteen feet six inches. In this park one may wander in summer into lovely nooks, overshadowed by oaks and beeches, with softest mosses, turf and wild flowers to rest on, and fresh scents of lime leaves and grass stealing on the air, while the song of birds and the murmur of the little river Lodden charms the ear.

From *Picturesque England*, 1880

RIGHT: The Elm Avenue at Farnham Park in 1895.

ABOVE: The Lime and Beech Avenue in 2008.

The Preston Twins

PRESTON PARK, BRIGHTON, EAST SUSSEX 72

On the approach to Brighton from the north, you become aware of an abundance of Elm trees as you cross the South Downs. Whereas outside the area, Elms are few and far between, within the city boundaries up to 15,000 mature trees stand tall. Most European cities are adorned with London Plane trees, but here Elms are the order of the day. Many were planted in Georgian times when the city became a fashionable seaside resort, as Elms were pleasing to the eye and coped well with the harsh sea air.

At Preston Park, Brighton boasts the two largest and oldest English Elms in Europe. Known as the 'Preston Twins', they stand majestically together, each 6.38m (20.93ft) in girth and completely hollow. At around 500 years old, they remain in remarkably good health.

On 5 May 2009, two young Elms, brought in from Hyde Park, were planted adjacent to the pair, ensuring that the legacy continues should anything untoward happen to Brighton's favourite twins.

ABOVE: One of the Preston Twins with St Peter's Church visible behind, c. 1920.

Dutch Elm Disease

Dutch Elm Disease, or DED as it is sometimes called, is believed to have come to Britain on infected rock elm timber imported from North America around 1967, not from Holland as one might expect. A microfungal disease, it is carried by the elm bark beetle, which feeds on the wood beneath the bark, spreading the disease as it moves between the trees.

Earlier attacks of Dutch Elm Disease were reported in 1927 and again in the 1940s, but they were by no means as virulent and destructive as the outbreak that occurred in the 1960s. Twenty-five million Elms were felled nationwide in an attempt to halt the disease, which, while implemented with good intentions, had the effect of devastating our native Elm population.

At Brighton, however, the local authority took an altogether different approach towards combating DED, and decided to prune out infected branches at the first sight of infection, set bait traps for the beetles at the city limits and dig trenches between neighbouring trees to prevent contagion through root contact. This, coupled with the natural barrier of the South Downs to the north, a prevailing southwesterly onshore wind and an early warning helpline diligently used by local residents enabled the region to retain most of its elm population.

In 1998 the National Council for the Conservation of Plants and Gardens recognised the valiant efforts of Brighton and Hove's Dutch Elm Disease Management by awarding the city status as holder of the National Elm Collection.

OPPOSITE: The Preston Twins in spring 2009.

Broadway Elms

WORTHING, WEST SUSSEX 73

These large elegant Elms marked the border of the Warwick Estate, making a fine entrance to the seaside town of Worthing. They were retained as a feature when the Brighton road was widened in 1901 and renamed the Broadway. The shops beside them were also built at this time and still stand today. The same cannot be said for the trees, however, which were removed in 1928, 13 years after this photograph was taken, following a controversial debate which argued that they might become unsafe 'sometime in the future'. The council voted by the narrowest of margins to remove them, leaving Worthing all the poorer without them.

Such was thy ruin music making Elm
The rights of freedom was to injure thine
As thou wert served so would they
  overwhelm
In freedoms name the little so would
  they over whelm
And these are knaves that brawl for
  better laws
And cant of tyranny in stronger powers
Who glut their vile unsatiated maws
And freedoms birthright from the
  weak devours.

To A Fallen Elm, John Clare (1793–1864)

ABOVE: Elms in the Broadway, Worthing, c.1915.

The Dancing Tree

At Moretonhampstead there used to be a stone cross, which was erected when Scraggy Street still belonged to the church, sometime before 1636. An elm seed germinated within the pedestal that held the cross and took root, eventually tearing its host apart, and, as it flourished, the tree became known as the 'Cross Tree'.

In 1799, a local man named John Hancock opened 'The London Inn and Tavern' near the tree and took it upon himself to pollard the Elm, transforming it into a punchbowl shape. Henceforth, it became known as the 'Punchbowl Tree'.

The tree was used for celebrations on occasions such as May Day, floored and seated on a platform for dancing and with a staircase for the assembly to ascend, which included dancing couples and an orchestra. This is when the tree acquired its current name of the 'Dancing Tree'. During the Napoleonic War in the early nineteenth century, captured French officers were held prisoner in Moretonhampstead and they would congregate here.

On 13 October 1891, a violent storm shook much of the canopy and part of the hollow trunk fell down. Despite repair, the Elm finally succumbed to another storm in 1903, and it was replaced in 1912 with a Copper Beech, which survives to this day.

Instead of putting up a May-pole then, and frolicking around it, in a Pixy ring, the young folk of Moreton have their frisks among the verdure, without dread of dewy feet or toes stuck in a mole hill. High up in the tree, which stand in an elbow of Scraggy Street, they hoist and fix a timber platform, strong enough to bear the vehemence of dancing feet not too aerial. The boughs of the patulous tree, above the hole, afford a noble amplitude; and a double ring of hay rope, woven fast around the branches, provides the most headlong couple with a chance of preserving their necks, when valuable.

From *Christowell: A Dartmoor Tale*, Richard Doddridge Blackmore, 1885

ABOVE: The Copper Beech in 2009.
LEFT: The Dancing Tree, Moretonhampstead, c.1910.

St Keyne's Well

LISKEARD, CORNWALL 75

St Keyne lived in the late fifth century and spent most of her life performing good deeds in the West Country before she retired to Cornwall where she made her home. She was one of 25 children who were born to Brychan Brycheiniog, King of Brecknockshire (Brecon in Wales), 16 of whom became saints.

She is said to have planted four trees around the well near Liskeard – an Oak, an Ash, an Elm and a Withy (Willow tree) – and blessed them. The roots of the trees themselves formed the arched roof of the well. Upon her death she was carried there and imparted power to the waters in an effort to redress the balance of power between men and women; she felt that the latter were hard done by.

ABOVE: The wife gets to the well first!

Whichever drank first of the water,
a man or his wife,
would have the mastery in their wedded life.

A well there is in the west country,
and a clearer one never was seen,
There is not a wife in the west country
But has heard of the Well of St Keyne.

An Oak and an Elm-tree stand beside,
And behind does an Ash-tree grow,
And a Willow from the bank above
Droops to the water below.

'...If the husband of this gifted well
Shall drink before his wife,
A happy man thenceforth is he,
For he shall be master for life.

'But if the Wife should drink of it first,
God help the Husband then!'
The Stranger stoopt to the Well of
*   St Keyne,*
And drank of the water again.

From *The Well of St Keyne*, Robert Southey, 1798

The trees were blown down in a great storm in November 1703, but around 1745 Jonathan Rashleigh replaced them with five new trees – two Oaks, two Ash trees and an Elm.

In 1882, only an Ash and an Elm survived, and by the time of the photograph taken in 1912 only the hollow Elm remained. The tree was damaged by gales in November 1929 and deemed unsafe by the highway authority, which felled it the following year. The well was completely rebuilt by The Liskeard Old Cornwall Society in 1936, and is still maintained by them, albeit without a tree.

Stories abound of people who have tried the effect of drinking the waters, and in 1798 the Poet Laureate Robert Southey wrote a poem entitled *The Well of St Keyne* (above right).

ABOVE: St Keyne's Well and the Elm photographed in 1912.
OPPOSITE: The same year in colour.

CHAPTER THREE
The Beech

Beech *(Fagus sylvatica)*

Autumnal trees, breezing gently, swaying sweetly;
Discarding your raiment so discreetly.
Your yearly ritual of deeply carpeting the ground
With resplendent colour, and without sound.
From *Autumn*, Pauline Hight

ABOVE: Beech leaves.

OPPOSITE: Autumn colour shock in Hertfordshire woodland.

Often called the 'White Lady of the Wood', the Beech justly deserves its title of 'Mother of the Forest', its tall, slender and elegant form providing dappled shade through a vivid green canopy in the summer months, and rich autumn hues in the fall.

The level sunshine glimmers with green light.
From *Fears in Solitude*, Samuel Taylor Coleridge, 1798

Not so long lived as the Oak but frequently sharing forests with it, the Beech survives naturally between 150 and 250 years, but its life span can be spectacularly enhanced by pollarding. The wood was utilised by 'bodgers', who crafted chair legs and spindles for Windsor chairs in the forests of Buckinghamshire and the Chiltern Hills.

Native mainly to the southeast of England, the Beech has been widely planted with many fine specimens thriving as far north as Scotland. Growing up to 40m (131ft) tall, the smooth silver-grey bark has encouraged people through the ages to carve their names upon it. In fact, the name itself derives from the Saxon *beoce* or *boc*, from where we also get the word 'book'. Beechen bark tablets were used in early writings – remembering the 'leaves' of a book, and the Latin *folium* (leaf) from which are derived 'foliage' and 'folio'.

Beech nuts, or 'mast', provide food for a variety of wildlife and were previously used as a nut substitute – even in baking – and the extracted oil is said to be as good, after ageing, as olive oil

141

Meikleour Beech Hedge

MEIKLEOUR, TAYSIDE 76

Standing 36.5m (119.7ft) tall at its northern end, and extending for 530m (579 yards) along the Perth to Blairgowrie road, the Meikleour Beech Hedge is officially the tallest Beech hedge in the world. It takes four men about six weeks to trim and re-measure the hedge once every 10 years, using hand-held equipment on hydraulic platforms.

It was laid out in 1745 by Jean Mercer and her husband, Robert Murray Nairne, to mark the eastern boundary of their land at Meikleour. Robert was killed the following year on 16 April, along with some of the men who had planted the hedge, at the Battle of Culloden, the decisive battle of the Jacobite uprising against the English. Between 1,500 and 2,000 men on the Scots side were killed or wounded in contrast to only 301 on the English side. Culloden was the last pitched battle to be fought on British soil. Grieving for her husband, Jean Mercer fled Meikleour to seek refuge in Edinburgh, leaving the hedge growing ever closer to the heavens – a fitting memorial to the fallen.

As a footnote, by marrying into the Mercer family, Robert appears to have inherited a curse that had been placed upon them about 100 years earlier. In the mid-seventeenth century, a groom of Sir James Mercer of Aldie was condemned to death and hung from a tree for stealing a bowl of corn. He uttered the curse that 'the Mercers would have no male heirs for 19 generations'. Sir James' sons, James and William, died heirless, William's daughter Jane bore a daughter Margaret, who, in turn, had a girl Emily Jane. She married Henry, the 4th Marquess of Lansdowne, and together they had a son, the 5th marquess, who was born in London in 1845, finally breaking the curse. Ironically, he had a successful career in parliament at Westminster, with the distinction of holding posts in both Liberal and Conservative governments.

...may justly be described as one of the arboreal wonders of the world.

From *Woods, Forests, and Estates of Perthshire*, Thomas Hunter, 1883

ABOVE: The Meikleour Beech Hedge in 2009, barely changed in over a century.

ABOVE: Beneath the canopy many of the Beech trunks are covered in graffiti.

ABOVE: The Meikleour Beech Hedge in 1905.

Burnham Beeches

BUCKINGHAMSHIRE

Further south at Burnham Beeches stands a remarkable collection of over 450 ancient pollarded trees. Of particular note are the old hollow Beeches. The 540-acre site is a legacy of a time gone by when trees were worked as a commodity. Trees were pollarded at around 2m (6.5ft) high (out of the reach of grazing animals) once every fifteen to twenty years, and they provided a source of timber for fuel and possibly fencing.

The very act of pollarding seems to fool the trees into thinking that they are younger than they are, thereby prompting regrowth and enabling them to survive to 500 years and beyond, whereas if it were left naturally to its own devices, a Beech would do well to live for more than 250 years.

In 1890, The City of London Corporation took ownership 'for the recreation and enjoyment of the people', thereby ensuring that the great trees would survive, as the entire area had been earmarked for development. Today, they are relearning by practical methods the ancient technique of pollarding, which has lapsed for over 150 years, as part of the continued management of the site.

The Romantic composer Felix Mendelssohn (1809–1847), was a frequent visitor to Burnham, and it is said to have inspired his incidental music for Puck and Oberon for *A Midsummer Night's Dream*. A Beech that was named after him blew down in 1990, but the stump was removed and now stands as a memorial at the Barbican in London.

There at the foot
of yonder nodding beech
That wreathes its old
fantastic roots so high,
His listless length at noontide
would he stretch,
And pore upon the brook
that babbles by.

From *Elegy Written in a Country Churchyard*, Thomas Gray, 1745

These lines were written about a particular tree at Burnham Beeches, later known as 'Gray's Beech', which he frequently visited.

OPPOSITE: Ancient pollard Beeches at Burnham in 2009.

ABOVE: A pollarded Beech in 1905.

His Majesty
BURNHAM BEECHES, BUCKINGHAMSHIRE 79

ABOVE: His Majesty photographed in 1933.
ABOVE LEFT: Burnham Beeches from *Picturesque England*, 1850.

The oldest and largest girthed Beech at Burnham was recorded in 1871 at a staggering 9.71m (31.85ft), but for many years 'His Majesty' ruled the roost. At 8.5m (27.8ft) 90cm (3ft) from the ground in 1931 – two years before the archive photograph (right) was taken – the tree was aptly named due to its huge size rather than in honour of a particular monarch. The giant Beech pollard was thought to be 600 years old when it was brought down in the hurricane of 1987, which was responsible for felling thousands of large trees – particularly Beech with their shallow root systems – across the southeast of England and beyond.

A new Beech tree was planted by the Lord Major of London in 1989 in order to mark the 800th anniversary of the mayorality of the City of London.

The King Beech
KNOLE PARK, KENT 80 🌿

Thomas Cranmer, one-time Archbishop of Canterbury and later Oxford Martyr, was the main protagonist of Henry VIII's plan to obtain support for the annulment of his marriage to Catherine of Aragon. However, he probably did not expect to be persuaded into giving his palace at Knole Park to the King. Henry spent plenty of money on the dwelling despite never residing there, and it was his daughter Elizabeth I who finally passed the estate on to the Sackville family whose descendents still live there.

That the King Beech was named after Henry is doubtful – the tree probably acquired its name due to its immense size, much like His Majesty at Burnham Beeches (see opposite) and the Queen Beech at Ashridge Park.

If we take the height of the iron fence around the tree in the archive photograph (right) to be 1.5m (4.9ft), then we can estimate the girth of the King Beech at its waist (the thinnest part – about the height of the fence) to be over 9m (29.5ft) in diameter. There is no doubt that the King Beech was certainly a giant.

Like many of its counterparts at Knole Park, however, the King Beech was lost in the great storm of October 1987.

ABOVE: The King Beech in 1905.
LEFT: Old Beech stump at Knole Park.

149

The Grand Avenue

SAVERNAKE FOREST, WILTSHIRE 81

Famed equally for its Beech trees as it is for its Oaks, Savernake hosts the longest tree-lined avenue in Britain. The Grand Avenue runs for 6.2km (3.9 miles) right through the centre of the forest. Laid out in 1790 by Capability Brown, the avenue is lined with hundreds of Beech trees and follows the path of the old Roman road from Tottenham House to Marlborough. Many of the trees were felled between 1980 and 1981, and it was replanted in 1983, so that a continuous line could be maintained.

To the southwest of the avenue stands the largest and most impressive Beech tree in the forest – the Great Beech. Standing tall with a girth of 5.91m (19.39ft) and an enormous spreading canopy, the giant shows no signs of slowing down, still dominating its domain.

ABOVE: The Grand Avenue in 1901.

LEFT: The Great Beech in 2009.

St John's Beech

There has been a church in Frome since St Aldhelm built a monastery there in AD685. The current building of St John's Church is mostly twelfth to fifteenth century, standing above St Aldhelm's spring, which runs down the medieval and picturesque Cheap Street in an open stream known as the 'leet'. Some Saxon carved stones are still visible inside the church – incorporated into an internal wall at some stage of rebuilding, and probably taken from a Saxon cross that stood in the locality.

The churchyard underwent a major restoration in 1854 by the Revd W J E Bennett; substantial re-bordering and the current layout were developed. The 5.5-m (18-ft) girthed Copper Beech tree at the eastern end of the churchyard where it meets Blindhouse Alley may have been planted at that time, but it is more likely that the tree was already standing. It exhibits all the attributes of an ancient Beech – a huge girth, hollowing and decay around the trunk and upper branches, playing host to several forms of fungi.

It has the appearance of a gnarled old elephant – the smooth grey trunk giving rise to a spread of branches, which supports a mammoth canopy. But the tree showed signs of disease within its trunk when analysed by local horticulturalists, and it could be nearing the end of its days if the local council follows its recent course of action of removing 'problem' town centre trees. A large Horse Chestnut, beloved of local schoolchildren for its conkers, was cut down and scrubbed out as it was deemed to have obscured the hallowed view of the CCTV cameras. Perhaps we should adjourn to the church to pray for the wellbeing of the elephant Beech.

ABOVE: St John's Beech in 2010.

151

Hatfield Forest

ESSEX

ABOVE: An ancient Hornbeam in Hatfield Forest, c.2005.

Previously part of the now diminished but once vast forest of Essex, Hatfield Forest was hunted by kings even before the Conquest. William the Conqueror took possession following Harold's defeat at Battle, and the forest remained in royal ownership until 1238. By 1304, it had passed into the hands of Robert the Bruce, but so busy was he north of the border that it is doubtful he ever enjoyed it. Edward I confiscated Bruce's lands, and Hatfield continued to pass between royal and private hands, following dispute after dispute, until 1924 when most of it came into the care of the National Trust. By 1946, the whole forest was under their stewardship. Hatfield's last red deer, hunted for centuries by the medieval kings, were killed during the First World War.

The forest has many fine Oak, Chestnut and Beech trees, but it is perhaps most renowned for its ancient Hornbeams. Often overlooked and mistaken for Beech and Elm, with whom it shares similar characteristics, the Hornbeam was favoured in history for its extremely hard timber and was extensively pollarded for fire wood and charcoal burning, where it excelled.

Native mainly to the southeast of England, the Hornbeam rarely grows above 30m (98.4ft), its fluted trunk and twisted branches distinguishing it from the Beech. The ability to retain its leaves makes it ideal for hedges, and it was the preferred tree for the bower avenues beloved of medieval queens.

Let beauteous hornbeams
one fair part adorn;
Another, cypresses with judgement shorn:
These mazy windings form a wilderness,
Which hornbeam hedges
in trim neatness dress.
Along the alley sides their boughs expand:
Like verdant walls
the firm espaliers stand;
And, while the eyes
their various forms delight,
To private walks
and shady bowers invite.

From *Hortorum Libri IV*, René Rapin, 1665 (translated from the Latin original)

ABOVE: A view under a sunlit Chestnut among the ancient trees of Hatfield Forest, c.2005.

OPPOSITE: An equally ancient Hornbeam in Hatfield Forest, c.2005.

CHAPTER FOUR

The Ash

Ash *(Fraxinus excelsior)*

OAK BEFORE ASH, IN FOR A SPLASH
ASH BEFORE OAK, IN FOR A SOAK.
TRADITIONAL SAYING

ABOVE: An old hedge Ash in Somerset, 2009.

OPPOSITE: A coppiced Ash left to regrow, its five stems supporting a makeshift tree house in Frome. It was felled in 2010 by developers.

The Ash, native to Britain and most of Europe, grows to 30m (98.4ft) tall, and, although it rarely lives for longer than 250 years, it does, on occasion, produce very ancient and large-trunked trees. Its leaves are pinnate: they are divided into nine to thirteen leaflets as opposed to the single broad leaves of the Oak, Elm and Beech.

Ash is generally held as providing the best firewood and it burns well even when it is green, so traditionally the tree has been coppiced or pollarded specifically for this purpose.

The Greeks believed their Meliae, deities of nature, were nymphs of the tree, and in Norse mythology, the Ash was held in the highest order, representing Yggdrasil – the world tree or tree of life, with its branches in the heights of heaven and its roots in the depths of hell. Yggdrasil supported the nine worlds and one could travel to each via its branches. On top of the tree perched a giant eagle, while the dragon Nidhogg gnawed at its roots, and along its trunk ran a squirrel Ratatosk, delivering insults to the pair. Four stags fed on its bark.

Odin, the Norse god of war, hung himself with his spear in his side (reminiscent of Christ's suffering on the cross) for nine days and nights from the branches of Yggdrasil in order to see the sacred runes and be filled with knowledge. In Anglo Saxon England he became Woden, who is still remembered in our calendar as Wednesday.

The name Ash comes from the old English *aesc*, meaning 'spear', as does its Latin name of *fraxinus* – perhaps both are a reference to the tree's primary early use.

Gelert's Grave

BEDDGELERT, GWYNEDD 83 🌿 🍃

Llewelyn the Great (1172–1240) was a Welsh prince who took control of the whole of Gwynedd by the time he was only 27 years old. He laid the strong foundations for his grandson Llewelyn the Last through a combination of war and diplomacy. He also built a strong relationship with King John of England, marrying his illegitimate daughter Joan in 1205, and fighting in his campaign against the Scots. However, the relationship turned sour within a decade, and Llewelyn found himself on the losing side of a battle when John invaded in 1211, forcing him to give up his eastern lands and make terms.

Within three years, however, Llewelyn regained his lands by using his army, and extended his kingdom south, gaining support from the many Welsh who were opposed to John, who had by now signed Magna Carta.

The prince had a palace at Beddgelert in Snowdonia, where he held hunting parties. Legend says his prize hunting dog, Gelert, blessed with a presentiment of danger and thought to have been given to Llewelyn by King John himself, was missing on one such occasion. The prince returned home in search of the hound, so unusual was his absence, and on arrival was greeted by a happy dog. But the Greyhound's coat was streaked with blood, whereupon Llewelyn entered his chambers to find his baby son missing from an upturned and bloodstained cot. In an act of impulsive revenge, the prince thrust his sword into the side of Gelert, thinking the hound had killed his son – but the dog's death cry was answered by the cry of a baby. Llewelyn saw the boy alive and well, lying beside the large dead wolf that Gelert had killed in his defence. Filled with remorse, Llewelyn ordered the burial of his dog with full honours at Beddgelert and is said never to have smiled again. The place is apparently named after the incident – Beddgelert translates as Gelert's Grave.

The basic substance of the story appears in many cultures across the world, offering the moral 'think twice before you act in haste'. This has led historians to question its validity and most now agree that the story of Gelert has earlier origins, which were attached to Beddgelert in the eighteenth century.

Local innkeeper David Prichard moved to the parish from south Wales around 1793 and founded the Royal Goat Hotel. A gregarious raconteur, he entertained the poet William Spencer with the story of Gelert on a visit in 1800. Spencer was sufficiently taken with the tale to compose one of his most famous works, *Beth Gelert*, or 'The Grave of the Greyhound', shortly afterwards. In an effort to attract visitors and boost his takings, it is thought that Prichard married the tale with that of his village, simply naming the dog Gelert. In 1802, he erected a stone boulder and slabs engraved with the story on the mound.

A large Ash tree grew from the enclosed mound, which lies in a field in the shadow of the mountain Y Lliwedd. It appears as a mature but windswept tree in the archive photograph – there is no doubt as to the direction of the prevailing wind – and, judging by its size, could have been planted around the same time that the stones were laid, but the tree died and was replaced by the Sycamore and Copper Beech that remain today.

So if the Gelert in the village name did not have its origins in the hound story, who is it named after? Evidence points to a late seventh-century saint called Celer, who lived in a cave near Llandysul, 109km

(68 miles) from Beddgelert, where pilgrims travelled to be cured of their ills. An early Christian, Celer is thought to have worked as a missionary in Beddgelert and he was martyred there.

The remains of famed Cylart,
*   so faithful and good,*
*   The bounds of the cantred conceal;*
Whenever the doe or the stag he pursued,
*   His master was sure of a meal.*

From *Musical Relicks of the Welsh Bards,* E Jones, 1784

RIGHT: Gelert's Grave with plaque, 2009.
BELOW: Gelert's Grave and Y Lliwedd, 1905.

The Wesley Tree
WINCHELSEA, SUSSEX 84

John Wesley was born in Epworth, Lincolnshire, in 1703, the son of a rector. He is best remembered as the founder of the Methodist movement – an evangelical branch of the Church of England – with his brother Charles.

Educated at Oxford, where he remained as a teacher, Wesley was ordained as a preacher in 1725, venturing to America ten years later with his brother Charles to lead a ministry in Georgia. He returned to England in 1738 and found great opposition to his methods from the established clergy. They not only disliked his passionate sermons but also took offence to his encouragement of preachers who had not been ordained. Wesley soon found himself with nowhere to practise, so he built the first Methodist chapel in Bristol and took to preaching in the open air, often beneath mature trees, which became known as 'Gospel Trees'.

He travelled around the country on horseback, spreading the word of God, and is said to have covered 250,000 miles. He had 300 lay preachers to further his cause, thus ensuring the expansion and future of Methodism.

There are an Elm tree at Stony Stratford, Buckinghamshire, clinging to life with a girth of 7.5m (24.6ft), and a 6.7-m (21.9-ft) Oak at Peckforton, Cheshire, that both bear his name, having been Gospel Trees where he preached, as well as a Yew at Lisburn where he 'preached at eight to a lively congregation, under the venerable old yew, supposed to have flourished in the reign of King James, if not of Queen Elizabeth' in 1778.

However, it is a large Ash tree at Winchelsea in Sussex that is most famous for bearing Wesley's name. This is the place where he delivered his final open-air sermon on 7 October 1790, six months prior to his death at the age of 87. He described the place as 'that poor skeleton of ancient Winchelsea' and he had to perform the service sitting down, such was his age.

The tree toppled over in a storm in 1927, much weakened from souvenir hunters, but a cutting was taken from which a new tree was grown and planted in its place in 1931. That tree still stands.

I stood under a large tree and called to most of the inhabitants of the town 'the kingdom of heaven is at hand: repent and believe in the Gospel'. It seemed as if all that heard were, at the present, almost persuaded to be Christians.

John Wesley on his last sermon

ABOVE: *Wesley's Tree* from a watercolour by W H Borrow (1863–1893).

OPPOSITE: Re-enactment of John Wesley's last open air sermon beneath the replacement ash by residents and members of the Friends of Wesley's Chapel, 2006.

CHAPTER FIVE

The Lime

Lime *(Tilia)*

THE LINDEN BROKE HER RANKS AND RENT
THE WOODBINE WREATHS THAT BIND HER,
AND DOWN THE MIDDLE, BUZZ! SHE WENT,
WITH ALL HER BEES BEHIND HER.
FROM *AMPHION*, ALFRED, LORD TENNYSON (1809–1892)

ABOVE: The winged fruit and leaves of the Lime tree

OPPOSITE: A 6.45-m (21.16-ft) girthed Lime at Dinton Park, Wiltshire, 2008.

There are three kinds of Lime tree that are native to Britain: the broad-leaved (Tilia platyphyllos); small-leaved (Tilia cordata); and a hybrid of the two – the common Lime (Tilia x europaea). The tree grows to a stately height of 40m (131ft) and was widely planted from the seventeenth century onwards, flourishing in towns and parks, and tolerant to pruning. Some ancient coppiced Lime stools are thought to rank amongst the oldest broad-leafed trees in Britain.

The name derives from *lind*, the Saxon word for both 'smooth' and 'shield' – a purpose for which the timber was well used, utilising its ability to absorb a blow. The flowers attract bees in abundance, and can be used for making lime tea.

The stately lime, smooth, gentle, straight and fair,
With which no other Dryad can compare.
With verdant locks and fragrant blossoms deck't.
Does a large, even, oderate shade project.

Anonymous

161

Clumber Park Lime Avenue

WORKSOP, NOTTINGHAMSHIRE 85 🌿 🍃

Set on the northern edge of Sherwood Forest, Clumber was mentioned as early as 1076 in the *Domesday Book*, serving as a monastic settlement. Successive Dukes of Newcastle made it their princely home, but the last mansion to stand there was demolished in 1938 as part of an extreme tax-saving measure, eight years before the National Trust bought the 3,800-acre estate in 1946.

An impressive double avenue of Limes, lining each side of the drive from the entrance to the park, is the longest of its kind in Europe. It was planted around 1840 by W S Gilpin, an artist turned landscape gardener who was much sought after for landscape advice at around this time, and is almost 3.2km (2 miles) long, consisting of 1,296 common Limes – a fitting entrance to a grand estate.

In 1906, the trees suffered from insect attack, and bands of black grease were painted round their trunks in an effort to trap the insects, the marks of which are still visible today.

ABOVE: The Clumber Lime Avenue in 1912.

Landscape-gardeners, to insure success and confidence in their works, must be landscape-painters, in order to harmonize the colours and the groups of the trees with the buildings, and the natural features of the landscape around them.

From *The Quarterly Journal of Agriculture Vol III*, submission by W S Gilpin, 1831

ABOVE: The Clumber Lime Avenue, c.2005.

CHAPTER SIX

The Scots Pine

Scots Pine *(Pinus sylvestris)*

ABOVE: Pine flower.
OPPOSITE: In the Blackwood of Rannoch, 2009.

The Scots Pine is the only Pine tree native to Britain – one of the first trees to colonise the island following the retreat of the last ice age some 10,000 years ago. Later came the native broadleaf trees, such as the Beech and Oak, which eventually dominated in England, but in Scotland vast swathes of Pine, which were known famously as the Caledonian Forest, covered the land.

Growing to a height of up to 36m (118ft) and a girth of 3.5m (11.4ft), the Scots Pine can live for between 250 and 300 years, but one recent discovery in Caledonia was found to be over 520 years old.

The Druids decorated Pine groves with stars and lights reflecting their ritual fires at the winter solstice to entice the sun back – an obvious precursor to our modern-day Christmas tree. The Romans used the fruit of the tree, the pine cone, to flavour their wine; hence the *thyrsus*, or wand, in the hands of their god Bacchus (Greek Dionysus), topped with a pine cone, which was thought to represent fertility.

The straight growth of younger Pines made its timber ideal for planking and ships' masts. The masts of *HMS Discovery* – Captain Scott's famous vessel, which carried him and his heroic but ill-fated crew to the Antarctic – were made from Caledonian Pine trees.

In the eighteenth and nineteenth centuries, Pine stands were planted in England by wealthy landowners to benefit their offspring, as a good crop could be yielded in only 50 years. A legacy of this practice are the many Pines found around England today, long held to be beneficial for respiratory complaints.

The Blackwood of Rannoch

PERTHSHIRE

Nestled on the southern banks of Loch Rannoch and covering an area just 4.8km (3 miles) wide, the Blackwood of Rannoch is the most southerly remnant of Scotland's ancient Caledonian Forest. Much of the country was once covered in a dense growth of Pine, Birch and Rowan, vast tracts of which have been successively felled or burnt over millennia. It is estimated that only one per cent of the original forest survives today in 35 isolated locations. Various projects are underfoot to restore the Caledonian Forests to their former glory, but, clearly, there is still a long way to go.

Canals are still visible in the centre of the forest and were cut in the seventeenth century to carry felled timber down to the loch below. Further felling was carried out during the Second World War by the Canadian Forestry Corps to aid the war effort.

The forest supports a wide range of wildlife, including the golden eagle, which roosts in the pine canopy, red squirrel, pine marten, mink, wildcat, fox and deer, although the latter are controlled by shooting as they are thought to hinder regeneration of the Pines when grazing. Black grouse and capercaillie, which were reintroduced in 1837 following their extinction in the eighteenth century, feed on the buds and shoots of the Pines. Wood ants, lichens and fungi are also prevalent. Previously, wild boar, beavers, lynx, moose, brown bears and wolves lived in the forest, but were hunted to extinction – the last wolf being shot in 1743.

ABOVE: An ancient Scots Pine at Rannoch School, bordering the western edge of the Blackwood, c.1930.

OPPOSITE: The Blackwood of Rannoch in 2009.

BELOW: The Blackwood of Rannoch in 2009.

Gunnar's Tree

THE BLACKWOOD OF RANNOCH, PERTHSHIRE 86

On the brow of a hill near a pathway that runs through the Blackwood of Rannoch stands Gunnar's Tree, an ancient Scots Pine with a girth of 4.27m (14ft). It was named at a special ceremony in 2000 to commemorate 25 years since the Blackwood was designated a Forest Reserve – a Special Area of Conservation (SAC), thereby ensuring its survival for the future.

A plaque was set on stone and was placed at the foot of Gunnar's Tree to celebrate the life of Gunnar Godwin and to recognise his contribution towards saving the Blackwood.

Born in Grimsby in 1915 of Danish and Icelandic parents, Gunnar became a Forestry Commission Conservator for East Scotland and played a key role in campaigning for the importance of the ancient Caledonian wood. Up until this point, not many people had seen the value of the historic forest, and it was in very real danger of being lost.

Even now developers periodically try to encroach on the area, set as it is on the banks of Loch Rannoch, a site of great beauty. In 2010, permission was denied for the development of a hotel complex and golf course at Rannoch School, Dall, which borders the Blackwood. I helped to campaign against the application following a visit in 2009. For now, at least, the future of the Blackwood seems secure.

OPPOSITE: Gunnar's Tree in 2009.

BELOW: Gunnar's commemoration plaque.

CHAPTER SEVEN

The Yew

Common Yew (*Taxus baccata*)

OLD EMPEROR YEW, FANTASTIC SIRE,
GIRT WITH THY GUARD OF DOTARD KINGS,
WHAT AGES HAST THOU SEEN RETIRE
INTO THE DUSK OF ALIEN THINGS?
WHAT MIGHTY NEWS HATH STORMED THY SHADE,
OF ARMIES PERISHED, REALMS UNMADE?
FROM *THE FATHER OF THE FOREST*, WILLIAM WATSON, 1895

ABOVE: Yew flowers.
OPPOSITE: A stand of Yews, 2010.

If the Oak is the king of the forest, then the Yew tree is the old grandfather. This is our longest-lived tree, surviving sometimes beyond 4,000 years, and we are lucky enough in Britain to have both the best and most plentiful ancient examples in Europe due in equal measure to both war and religion.

The Yew was revered by the pagan priesthood of Druids, who used its groves for their sacred ceremonies. When Christianity replaced the old religion, many of these sites were re-used, the significance of the tree living on as a symbol of eternal life, representing the Tree of Life in the Garden of Eden. Yew has the ability to regenerate, often filling its own hollow trunk with new growth, and re-rooting itself to start new trees when its drooping boughs meet the earth.

When England went to war in the Middle Ages, the longbow was the weapon of choice, but European yew was found to be superior for bow making to English yew, which, in turn, led to the devastation of the species on the continent. That, in tandem with the preservation of Yews in our churchyards, where a tree was traditionally planted when a new church was built, is where we find most specimens today.

The tree is poisonous, with the exception of the red arils that harbour the seeds and which are very toxic (the word comes from the Latin name for the tree – *taxus*). Traditional folk remedies sometimes resulted in fatalities, but young needles have recently been used in a chemotherapy treatment for cancer, fuelling the Yew's reputation as a life giver and lending some credence to the old wives' tales.

171

The Fortingall Yew

FORTINGALL, PERTHSHIRE 87

What better place to start this chapter than with the Fortingall Yew? Not only is the tree reputed to be the oldest Yew in Britain but it is also the oldest living organism in Europe. It sits in the churchyard of Fortingall in Perthshire, and estimates have put it at between 2,000 and 5,000 years old – I'll go with the popular assumption of 4,000 years. This would make it older than the nearby Bronze Age tumulus, perhaps predating the pagan harvest festival of Samhain, (today largely replaced by Halloween), which was held in the village up until 1924. No doubt the church was built here to absorb these pre-Christian beliefs and replace the influence of the stone circle in the field beyond.

Oral tradition cites Fortingall as the birthplace of Pontius Pilate, the Roman procurator in Judea from AD26–36. Caesar Augustus certainly sent an embassy to Scotland before the invasion of Britain in AD55, one of the ambassadors being Pilate's father. The Romans were conducted to the nearby residence of Metallanus, king of Caledonia. This could conceivably have led to a meeting of Pilate's father with a Scottish woman, making Pontius a Romano-Scot.

Metallanus's successor, Caractacus, the British freedom fighter, fought a fierce battle with Agricola, a Roman general responsible for much of the Roman conquest of Britain, on this very spot. The Yew would have been of significant size even then, 2,000 years ago.

The once-vast creature was measured at 15.85m (52ft) by Daines Barrington in 1769, but it suffered at the hands of relic hunters over the centuries to such a degree that its remaining stems appear as several small trees. Now protected by a stone wall, the tree remains in reasonably good health, offering abundant foliage. Cuttings taken by the Forestry Commission are to be propagated with a view to planting them around the country. In this way, the gene pool of the Fortingall Yew is set to survive for perhaps several more millennia to come.

OPPOSITE: Remains of the trunk in 2009. The pegs mark the previous girth of the tree.

ABOVE: *The Great Yew at Fortingall* by J G Strutt, 1822.

ABOVE: The Fortingall Yew in 1905.

ABOVE: The Fortingall Yew in 2009.

The Borrowdale Yews

SEATHWAITE, CUMBRIA 88

Where there are now three ancient Yews forming a famous grove at Seathwaite in the hills of Borrowdale, there used to be four. One was lost in a storm in 1883, but this seems to be just a part of their long evolutionary tale. The largest of the trees is known as the Borrowdale Yew and stands with a girth of 7.56m (24.8ft), although it was doubtless much larger than that in previous years. The battered, hollow trunk has been at the mercy of the elements for centuries, living in England's wettest climate.

The female Yew lost a large branch during a fierce storm in January 2005, reducing the crown to half of its previous size, but by dendrochronology the branch was shown to have 1,500 annual growth rings, giving some idea of the great age of the tree, the trunk itself being much older than its crown. Hundreds of trees fell in the area during the storm.

The two smaller Yews further down the hill have around half the girth of their mother tree at 4.27m (14ft) and 4.5m (14.7ft) respectively, but rather than being grown by seed there is a theory that they could be attached by a common root system, making the grove one huge regenerative organism. Yews often re-root when drooping branches meet the soil, forming new trees that are still very much part of the parent.

When Wordsworth visited the grove, immortalising them in his poem Yew Trees in 1803, he may well have shown insight ahead of his time by describing the trees fraternally.

With harsher winters and more localised damaging storms, the Yews at Borrowdale stand to have no easier time of it in the future, but the National Trust, which cares for the Lake District, resolved to leave them to care for themselves. Not a bad policy considering the little help they have needed over the last 2,000 years.

RIGHT: The Borrowdale Yew, c.2005.
OPPOSITE: The Borrowdale Yews, evening, 1908.

But worthier still of note
Are those Fraternal Four of Borrowdale
Joined in one solemn
  and capacious grove;
Huge trunks!
  and each particular trunk a growth
Of intertwisted fibres serpentine.

From *Yew Trees*, **William Wordsworth, 1803**

The Yewdale Monarch

CONISTON, CUMBRIA 89 🌿

Yew Tree Farm took its name from the ancient Yewdale Monarch, already 500 years old when the farmhouse was built in 1693 and where the Walker family lived for over 200 years. However, the farm probably owes its fame to the celebrated children's writer Beatrix Potter, who purchased the estate in 1930 to save it from development. She sold half of the estate to the National Trust until they could afford to take it into their care completely. The tree was felled in 1896 when it was 700 years old, having grown to 8m (26.2ft) in girth. The old stump remains, rotting slowly in a field behind the farmhouse. A young Yew grows nearby.

*Nay, Traveller! rest. This lonely
  Yew-tree stands
Far from all human dwelling:
  what if here
No sparkling rivulet spread the
  verdant herb?
What if the bee love not these
  barren boughs?
Yet, if the wind breathe soft,
  the curling waves,
That break against the shore,
  shall lull thy mind
By one soft impulse saved from
  vacancy.*

From *Lines Left upon a Seat in a Yew-tree in Cumbria* by William Wordsworth, 1795

LEFT: The Yewdale Monarch, an engraving from *Picturesque Europe, c.*1850

The Yewdale Giant

Whilst on the subject of giants, it is worth mentioning a folk tale about the giant of Yewdale. Known as Will of the Tarns, he came to live in the area and was appreciated for his labouring skills. That is until he saw Lady Eva le Fleming out walking with her maid Barbara, whom he abducted and carried in his arms into the woods.

Horsemen attempted a rescue only to see Will throw Barbara into the river once he was cornered. The maid's lover dived in to save her but the pair were drowned. Small consolation then that the giant was slain on the spot.

RIGHT: The Yewdale Giant.

Fountains Abbey Yews

RIPON, YORKSHIRE 90

In October 1132, a disagreement and subsequent riot at St Mary's Abbey in York led to the exile of thirteen monks. The Archbishop of York, Thurstan, took them into his care and, at Christmas, he provided them with some land at Skelldale, near Ripon – a secluded and wooded valley with a river running through it from east to west. Thurstan thought it was the ideal place for the purpose of creating a new monastery.

The land was described as 'more proper for a retreat for wild beasts than the human species'. However, this did nothing to deter the monks who set to work at once, sheltering below the branches of a large Elm tree. But the winter weather forced them to move beneath the shade of seven Yew trees of immense size, growing on the south side of the valley. There the monks resided until they had completed building the monastery.

By the mid-fifteenth century one of the trees had blown down in a storm, by which time the monastery had become one of the most prosperous in England. The largest of the remaining trees was measured at 8m (26.2ft) in girth in 1658, J G Strutt noting them in 1823. However, according to John Lowe, only three still stood in 1891, a pair lying dead where they fell. On the south side of the River Skell, a 6.32-m (20.73-ft) girthed yew still stands.

With the dissolution of the monasteries by Henry VIII came the end of the line for Fountains as a practising monastery, and its only inhabitants today are a protected species of bat.

ABOVE: *Fountains Abbey Yew*, an engraving from 1845.

BELOW: The ruins at Fountains Abbey from the south bank of the River Skell with a Yew in the foreground.

177

Skipton Castle Yew
SKIPTON, YORKSHIRE 91 🍃

Built soon after 1090 to fend off raids from the marauding Scots, Skipton Castle is probably best remembered as the last northern stronghold of the English Civil War. In 1642, a 300-strong garrison, which was led by Sir John Mallory in support of King Charles I, withstood a Parliamentarian siege for three years before finally surrendering to Cromwell's men. The Royalists were allowed to march from the castle with full arms and colours in honour of their endeavour, but Cromwell still ordered that the stronghold should be 'slighted', removing the castle roofs.

Between 1657 and 1658, Lady Anne Clifford had the castle restored, and in 1659 she planted a Yew tree in Conduit Courtyard – so named after the spring that flowed there – to mark the occasion. Over 350 years later, the tree stands tall, with a girth of 2.75m (9ft), little changed from the photograph taken in 1893.

OPPOSITE: The Skipton Castle Yew in 1893.
BELOW: The Skipton Castle Yew in 2009.

The Betty Kenny Tree

SHINING CLIFF WOOD, AMBERGATE, DERBYSHIRE 92

ABOVE: The Betty Kenny Tree in 2008.

ABOVE: The Betty Kenny Tree, c.1920.

Kate and Luke Kenyon were charcoal burners at Shining Cliff Wood during the 1700s. They lived in what became known as 'The Betty Kenny Tree' ('Betty Kenny' was a local name for Kate Kenyon), a huge Yew that was believed to be around 2,000 years old. It was common at the time for charcoal workers to live in the woods where they worked, but not usually within the trees themselves! The Kenyons had eight children and a bough was hollowed out to act as a cradle for them. Legend holds that this is the origin of the nursery rhyme 'Rock a bye baby'.

The entire family savings of £5 were once stolen from the tree whilst the Kenyons were out in the forest working. The Kenyons were favoured by the Hurt family, who owned the wood and they commissioned the artist James Ward of the Royal Academy to paint a portrait of them. Kate lived to a ripe old age and danced at a party held in her honour at the Hurts' house on her 100th birthday. The dead Yew tree remains, despite being severely fire-damaged in the 1930s. In its prime, it had an estimated girth of 8m (26.2ft).

Rock a bye baby on the tree top,
When the wind blows
* the cradle will rock,*
When the bough breaks
* the cradle will fall,*
And down will come baby,
* cradle and all.*

Nursery rhyme

OPPOSITE: The Betty Kenny Tree, c.1920.

The Much Marcle Yew
MUCH MARCLE, HEREFORDSHIRE 93

Thought to be 1,500 years old, the Much Marcle Yew stands tall in St Bartholomew's churchyard with a girth of 9.31m (30.54ft). In 1953, it was measured at 9.14m (29.98ft), meaning that it grew by 17cm (7in) in 53 years, quite an achievement for an ancient Yew. The hollow trunk has been fitted with a bench where eight people can sit – look straight up and you can see clouds passing overhead.

Six tons of timber were removed from the tree in 2006 in an effort to lighten its load, but some of the Victorian lampposts that were used to support its drooping branches are still in place and the tree has changed little in over a century.

There are concerns over soil compaction around its roots due to large numbers of visitors, but the Much Marcle Yew is doing well and still lives up to Arthur Mee's description, written for The King's England in 1939, of an 'amazing veteran, a vigorous yew with a spread of branches 70ft across'.

ABOVE: The Much Marcle Yew in 2008.
BELOW: The Much Marcle Yew, c.1890.

Tallest Yew Hedge

CIRENCESTER, GLOUCESTERSHIRE 94

According to *The Guinness Book of World Records*, the Yew Hedge at Cirencester is the tallest of its kind in the world. It is 137m (450 ft) long, 10m (32.8ft) wide, 12m (39.3ft) tall and over 300 years old. It was planted by the 1st Earl of Bathurst around 1710 when he set about creating Cirencester Park, which he continued to plant enthusiastically with a wide variety of trees and shrubs for the next 65 years until his death in 1775, aged 90.

Every July, two workmen cut back 15cm (6in) of new growth over a two-day period, using a 21.3-m (70-ft) cherry picker. It would have taken the three men in the photograph considerably longer with hand shears back in the 1960s. The ton of clippings is sold on to pharmaceutical companies, which extract a chemical used in chemotherapy to fight breast, lung and ovarian cancer.

ABOVE: The 300-year-old Yew hedge in 2009.

RIGHT: Workers clipping the tallest Yew Hedge in the world in 1963.

The Ankerwyke Yew

ANKERWYKE ISLAND, BERKSHIRE 97

Two thousand years ago, this ancient Yew could well have been used in ritual worship by the Druids, who are known to have revered Yews as sacred trees. One thousand years later, anchorites resided near its shade, a monastic convent being founded by them around 1160. However, its crowning glory and place in history came on 15 June 1215, when King John famously signed the Magna Carta – the closest these islands have ever come to a constitutional bill of rights – within earshot of this very spot.

ABOVE: Ankerwyke Island from *Picturesque Europe*, 1850.

The Yew sits on Ankerwyke Island and is bounded by the River Thames on two sides, with inlets of water on the other two. It can be reached on foot by a narrow isthmus and is secluded to the point that it evokes a lost world or secret garden atmosphere.

Henry VIII is said to have wooed Anne Boleyn under its shade while she lived nearby at Staines. It evidently brought no luck or, for that matter, longevity to their union, as she was beheaded in 1536, Henry claiming the marriage to be the product of witchcraft.

In 1806, Dr Samuel Lyons measured the tree's girth at around 9m (over 30ft). By 2007, it was nearer 8m (26.2ft), so it is probably in a state of decay, but to say it has stopped growing would be a mistake – two of the branches droop to the ground where they have re-rooted and started new trees, while still attached to their parent, and the once-hollow trunk is almost filled with its own root growth, confirming the Yew's remarkable ability to regenerate over millennia. Tree ring analysis on a fallen branch showed it to be at least 335 years old, the tree itself being much older.

On my visit in 2008, I found the tree decorated with ribbons and decked with small garlands of flowers, echoing the pagan offerings that it may have witnessed 2,000 years ago.

What scenes have pass'd, since first this ancient Yew
In all the strength of youthful beauty grew!
Here patriot Barons might have musing stood,
And plann'd the Charter for their Country's good;
And here, perhaps, from Runnymede retired,
The haughty John, with secret vengeance fired,
Might curse the day which saw his weakness yield
Extorted rights in yonder tented field.
Here too the tyrant Henry felt love's flame,
And, sighing, breathed his Anne Bolyn's name;
Beneath the shelter of this Yew-tree's shade,
The royal lover woo'd the ill-starr'd maid:
And yet that neck, round which he fondly hung,
To hear the thrilling accents of her tongue;
That lovely breast, on which his head reclined,
Form'd to have humanized his savage mind;
Were Doom'd to bleed beneath the tyrants steel,
Whose selfish heart might doat, but could not feel.
O had the Yew its direst venom shed,
Upon the cruel Henry's guilty head,
Ere Englands sons with shuddering grief had seen
A slaughter'd victim in their beauteous queen!

From *Sylva Britannica*, Jacob Strutt, 1826

OPPOSITE: The Ankerwyke Yew viewed from a fallen branch in 2008.

The Druid's Grove

NORBURY PARK, DORKING, SURREY 98

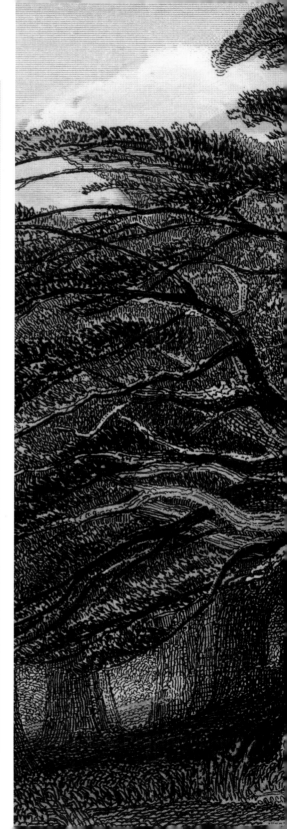

It has long been held that the Druids preferred tree groves as their venue of choice for ritual and ceremony, and this grove of Yews in Norbury Park is testament to that. Mentioned in the *Domesday Book* of 1086, some of these trees are thought to be 3,000 years old, predating even the pagan priest's existence and harking back to the Bronze Age, in keeping with the North Burr earthworks from which the park took its name.

Standing on a steep incline high above the River Mole, the Druid's Grove once afforded fine views across the valley, but this is now obscured by forest regrowth, despite many trees suffering damage from the Burns Day storm in 1991. The Yews suffered most as the storm occurred in January – the broad-leaved trees, having shed their leaves, left the evergreen Yews exposed to the full brunt of the gale. Huge fallen trunks litter the forest floor, but many survive, having crashed and regrown where they fell, once more highlighting the Yew's extraordinary power of regeneration. Work is underway to clear excessive tree growth around the Druid's Grove, giving them more space to thrive.

Lying between Dorking and Leatherhead, Norbury was purchased by William Lock in 1774 and transformed into a landscaped park. The house is still privately owned, but most of the grounds are owned by the local council and remain open to the public with a cycle track and walks.

LEFT: The Druid's Grove in 2009.

RIGHT: *The Druid's Grove* engraved by Radclyffe after T Allom for *A Topographical History of Surrey*, 1850.

The Crowhurst Yew

CROWHURST, SURREY 99

The Crowhurst Yew stands in the churchyard of the twelfth-century St George's Church. Estimates of its age range from 2,000 to 4,000 years, putting it on a par with the Fortingall and Tisbury Yews as one of the oldest trees in Europe. Whatever its age, it certainly predates the church and, for that matter, Christianity itself, illustrating how pre-Christian sites were absorbed by the Church in order to supplant pagan beliefs and encourage religious conversion.

In 1820, while the Yew was being hollowed out by local villagers, a cannonball from the Civil War was found lodged within its bole. A table and benches were fitted, said to seat up to a dozen people for tea. They also attached a small, hinged door, which is now sealed shut by re-growth of the wood. Whether it was added to keep people in or out is uncertain.

In 1650, John Aubrey measured the tree at 9.27m (30.4ft). The *Gardener's Chronicle* of 1874 recorded it at 9.37m (30.74ft). In 1984, Allen Meredith measured it at 9.6m (31.49ft), and the most recent measurement is 9.61m (31.53ft). It has grown in girth by just over one-third of a metre in over 350 years – that's less than a millimetre a year.

ABOVE: The Crowhurst Yew in 1907.
OPPOSITE: The Crowhurst Yew in 2009.

The Tandridge Yew
TANDRIDGE, SURREY 100

Not far from Crowhurst in the churchyard of St Peter's stands the Tandridge Yew. Although not considered to be quite as old as the tree at Crowhurst, it has a huge hollow girth of 10.77m (35.33ft), attesting to its ancient origins.

Excavation of an early Saxon church beside it shows that the foundations were skewed and a small vault was built to avoid the tree's roots, so it may well have been of significant size and importance over 1,000 years ago. The church has left the Yew almost to its own devices – no props or fencing here – so it has been allowed to grow naturally and has developed quite distinctly in shape and proportion from its distinguished neighbour.

The tree was featured on a second-class postage stamp as part of a series to commemorate the Millennium.

BELOW: The Tandridge Yew in 2009.

The Selborne Yew

SELBORNE, HAMPSHIRE 101

ABOVE: The Monument Yew in 2009.

Estimates vary between 800 and 1,500 years as to the age of the ancient Yew in St Mary's churchyard, but the huge trunk points to a great age, possibly predating the twelfth-century church.

Selborne's most famous resident, the naturalist Gilbert White, was fond of the tree and measured its girth at 7m (22.96ft) in 1789. His body lies buried in the churchyard, marked by a simple stone inscribed 'G W 26th June 1793'. In 1901, F Southerden and Lewis Eynon remeasured the tree and found it to be 7.77m (25.49ft). In 120 years, it had grown only 1.39m (4.56ft).

Then, suddenly, at 3pm on 25 January 1990, the old tree came crashing down to the ground. It fell victim to the Burns Day Storm, having previously survived many others. Beneath its roots, burials were found dating to the fifteenth century – the tree had absorbed the graves over the centuries as it grew. The church and local people rallied and, after professional advice, decided to try and resurrect the great Yew. The lower branches were cut and a crane was used to haul the tree upright and back into position. After a while new growth appeared, but within a year the Selborne Yew was pronounced dead and now stands solemnly as a monument to its former glory.

ABOVE: The Selborne Yew and Trumpeter's Grave in 1907.

ABOVE: Gilbert White's drawing of the Selborne Yew, *c.* 1789.

The Trumpeter's Grave

A solitary grave takes pride of place beside the great Yew tree at Selborne. The stone is marked with a cross and is inscribed simply: 'The Trumpeter'. It marks the spot where local farm labourer John Newland is buried.

The story goes that Newland led the Selborne workhouse riot in 1830, blowing his horn as he went and heading a 300-strong mob in protest against unfair taxes in hard times. Encouraged by local farmers who were fed up with paying the shortfall for the local 'poor tax', the mob made their way to Selborne workhouse, turned out the owners and ransacked the place, evidently repulsed by the treatment of the residents inside.

In truth, Newland was held to be 'a quiet, inoffensive man, except when he had been drinking', according to evidence given at the trial that followed. He was probably cajoled into fronting the horde simply because he had a trumpet.

Nine of the rioters were sentenced to transportation and all but one sailed for Australia in the spring of 1831 never to return to England. Newland himself served six months' hard labour at the County Gaol in Winchester.

In 1868, he died aged 77, and, at the request of his daughter Eliza and son William, the vicar allowed him to be buried beside the famous Yew where the Trumpeter's Stone still stands to commemorate his life and deeds.

RIGHT: The Trumpeter's Grave in 2009.

The Twyford Yew
TWYFORD, HAMPSHIRE 102 🌿

With a girth of only 4.17m (13.68ft), the Yew in St Mary's churchyard is probably only around 500 years old, and it could have been planted when the church was rebuilt in 1402. It holds the honour of being the oldest clipped Yew in Britain, a tradition that has been bestowed upon it for several centuries at least. These days, however, the local council has to apply for planning permission to clip it, as it sits in a conservation area.

ABOVE: The Twyford Yew in 2010.

Twelve sarsen stones were discovered in the earlier Norman tower foundations when further rebuilding took place in 1878, and they remain in place. According to legend, they were located on a nearby hill before the first Saxon church was built, so although the Yew was planted in Christian times, the site itself was most likely used for pre-Christain worship.

One 7 October, sometime in the eighteenth century, William Davies, a local man who was riding across Twyford Down in thick fog, found himself in danger of falling into a chalk pit. He was saved by the sound of the church bells, which alerted him to change his course. As a mark of gratitude, he left in his will an endowment as recompense for pealers to ring the bells every 7 October, and this tradition is still borne out to this day.

Hail, honour'd tree! that rear'st thy cone shaped head,
Where calmly sleeping lie the village dead;
Whose fame's been spoken oft, yet never sung,
My simple muse her tuneful harp hath strung.

From *Lines on the Yew Tree in Twyford Churchyard*, C Gilbert, 1850

ABOVE: *The Twyford Yew* in a watercolour by J T Hart, 187

197

St Nicholas's Yew

BROCKENHURST, HAMPSHIRE 103 🌱

Standing in the churchyard of St Nicholas in Brockenhurst, the 6.66-m (21.85-ft) girthed tree (666 is an ominous number in Christian circles!) is the largest and oldest Yew in the New Forest, with a hollow trunk and a perfectly round hole straight through at its first bough.

Carbon dated in the mid-1980s at 1,000 years old, the ancient tree pre-dates the church, which was probably built on the site of a former pagan temple. Brockenhurst was the New Forest centre for hunting in medieval times, so British kings and queens through the ages would have undoubtedly worshipped here. Today, it sets a picturesque and peaceful scene.

...in the churchyard, spreads the gloom of a yew, which, from the Conqueror's day, to this hour, has darkened the graves of generations.

From *The New Forest: Its History and Its Scenery*, J R Wise, J R de Capel Wise, W Crane and W J Linton, 1863

ABOVE: St Nicholas's Yew, *c.* 1955, with an ancient Oak in the background – now gone.

OPPOSITE: St Nicholas's Yew in 2008.

The Wilmington Yew

WILMINGTON, SUSSEX 104

ABOVE LEFT: The Wilmington Yew in 1939.
ABOVE: The Long Man in 2009.
OPPOSITE: The Wilmington Yew in 2009.

The village of Wilmington sits in the shadow of the mysterious Long Man whose origins are still open to debate. Until recently it was thought to have been of at least Roman origin, but research that was carried out at Reading University places it firmly in the mid-sixteenth century and it could have been laid out by monks from the local priory.

There can be no doubt as to the antiquity of the great Yew tree in the nearby parish churchyard, however. With a girth of 8.5m (27.8ft) at 20cm (8in) from the ground and thought to be some 1,600 years old, this split tree marks an earlier pagan centre for worship in the village, a mantle that the Norman church took over 1,000 years ago.

Held aloft with numerous wooden props supporting its weary boughs, the tree has a large chain around its middle, but it has hardly changed in the half century between these photographs.

O not for thee the glow, the bloom,
Who changest not in any gale,
Nor branding summer suns avail
To touch thy thousand years of gloom.

From *In Memoriam A.H.H.*, **Alfred, Lord Tennyson,**1849

The Twin Yews

MELLS, SOMERSET 105

Legend ascribes the origin of the nursery rhyme Little Jack Horner firmly at the feet of the Horner family at Mells, although the family disputes this. By 1539, the only monastery to have escaped Henry VIII's dissolution was Glastonbury, but this was about to change. The Abbott of Glastonbury, Richard Whiting, was summoned to the Tower of London where Thomas Cromwell declared he should be executed at Glastonbury. Whiting had the foresight to entrust his steward Thomas Horner with twelve valuable deeds to various manors, which they hid in a Christmas pie – a common practice of the time to avoid theft. Horner took the pie to London with a view to appeasing the King, but, apparently realising the fruitlessness of his task, he opened the pie and kept the deeds to Mells Manor, the pick of the bunch, for himself. Thus the line 'pulled out a plum' is not only a play on words but also a reference to the Latin word *plumbum*, meaning 'lead', as the area was ripe for mining and could therefore provide good profits.

Another version of the story states that Horner paid a large sum to the King for the deeds in 1543. Either way, he was certainly no friend to the Abbott, and he sat on the jury that convicted him (on what charge remains unclear). Whiting was hung, drawn and quartered on Glastonbury Tor and the Abbey was destroyed.

A church certainly stood in Mells at this time, and the large twin Yew trees in the churchyard with girths of 4.4m (14.4ft) and 4.3m (14.1ft) suggest that they had already been planted.

A more recent Yew tree avenue, which was designed by Lutyens, stands behind the church, and the famous wartime poet Siegfried Sassoon lies buried in the churchyard.

Little Jack Horner sat in the corner
Eating his Christmas pie,
He put in his thumb
*   and pulled out a plum*
And said 'What a good boy am I!'.

Nursery rhyme

ABOVE: New Street leading to Mells Church and the Yews, *c.*1920.

OPPOSITE: The Twin Yews in 2011.

The Stoke Gabriel Yew

STOKE GABRIEL, DEVON 106

ABOVE LEFT: The Yew and church in 1910.

ABOVE: This photograph shows how the tree has barely changed in 80 years.

Nestled high on the northern bank of the River Dart, the Yew at Stoke Gabriel grows in the churchyard where a church has stood since the Norman Conquest, although the present one dates to the thirteenth and fifteenth centuries.

Estimates of the tree's age range from 800 to 1,500 years, but a girth of 5.03m (16.5ft) places it at the younger end of the scale. However, an old rhyme associated with the tree reads:

> *Walk ye backward round about me*
> *Seven times round for all to see*
> *Stumble not and then for certain*
> *One true wish will come to thee.*

An earlier fertility rite declared that fertility could be achieved by a woman if she walked forwards around the tree and for a man if he walked backwards around it, suggesting a memory of pre-Christian worship in the area, which has survived into recent times.

Next to the church stands Church Orchard, which is one of the last remaining ancient apple orchards in South Devon.

OPPOSITE: The Stoke Gabriel Yew, c. 1930.

The Wild Cherry

Wild Cherry (*Prunus avium*)

So we grew together,
Like to a double cherry, seeming parted;
But yet a union in partition,
Two lovely berries moulded on one stem.
From *A Midsummer Night's Dream*, William Shakespeare

ABOVE: Cherry blossom.

OPPOSITE: Cherry trees in blossom in April in Bohetherick Orchard, near Cotehele Quay, Cornwall. It is one of the few remaining Cherry orchards in the Tamar Valley.

Of Britain's three species of Cherry, the Wild Cherry, or gean as it is also known, grows the largest, sometimes to 30m (98.4ft) in height. Frequently planted, but often found in woodland where it thrives in the shade of larger trees such as the Beech, its purple-grey peeling bark and beautiful snow-white blossoms herald the arrival of spring. By summer, the large bronze, sharp-toothed leaves turn to pale green, and later to bright crimson in autumn. The heart-shaped bitter-sweet cherry fruits arrive in midsummer, changing in colour from yellow to red and then almost to black – beloved of birds.

The name 'cherry' originates from the Romans' *Cerasus*, since which time the tree has been abundantly planted and enjoyed for its aesthetic pleasure as much as for its fruit. In days gone by, cherries were sold in London to the shout of:

Cherry-ripe, ripe, ripe, I cry,
Full and fair ones; come and buy.

Furthermore, it is sometimes said that the number of cherries that are shaken from a tree by a child represents the years of its life.

Studley Royal Wild Cherry

RIPON, YORKSHIRE 107

When John Aislabie inherited the Studley Royal Estate in 1693, he set about landscaping the park in the style of the day, and this work was continued by his son John. In 1767, John purchased the adjoining grounds of Fountains Abbey, where the famous Yew trees stood. Between them, the Aislabies created one of the most important eighteenth-century water gardens in England, which remain today much as they were conceived over 300 years ago. The 360-acre park is still grazed by herds of deer, as it has been since medieval times.

At its centre stands one of the largest Wild Cherry trees in Britain, possessing a huge girth of 6.42m (21ft) at 1.3m (4.2ft) from the ground around its gnarled and fluted trunk. The Cherry lost its crown during a severe storm in 2008, but it remains an impressive sight, especially when it is flowering.

The National Trust purchased the Studley estate, along with Fountains Abbey, from North Yorkshire County Council in 1983, and it now cares for the Studley Royal Wild Cherry, along with some fine Oaks, Limes and Chestnuts.

RIGHT: The Studley Royal Wild Cherry in flower, 2010.

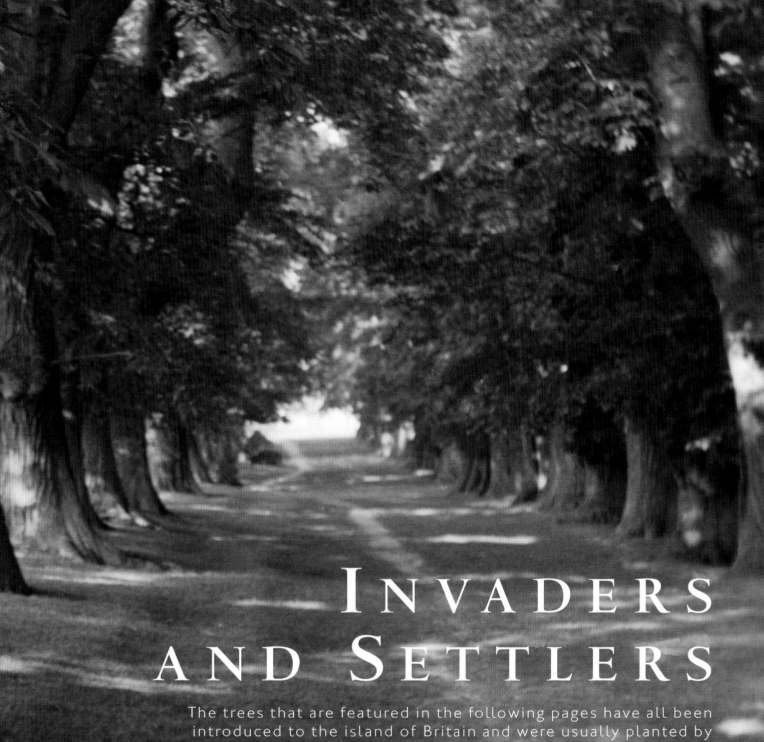

INVADERS
AND SETTLERS

The trees that are featured in the following pages have all been introduced to the island of Britain and were usually planted by invaders to our shores, travelling pilgrims or the great tree hunters of the sixteenth to nineteenth centuries.

CHAPTER SEVEN

The Apple

Wild Apple, Crab Apple
(Malus sylvestris)

ABOVE: Apple blossom in spring.
OPPOSITE: Apple fruits in autumn.

You may wonder why the Apple tree features in this part of the book, synonymous as it is with the very essence of Britain. It was revered by the Druids in their sacred orchards; it was beloved of medieval kings and queens; and it took centre stage in the ancient ritual of 'Wassailing', which is still practised in some Somerset villages.

Evidence suggests that the common apple in our fruit bowls and ciders is descended from a western Asian variety and was introduced to Britain by the Romans. Our native Wild Apple is the Crab Apple, which still grows in woods and hedgerows – too tart for our modern tastes but especially good in preserves and cider. The juice from the fruit is known as verjuice and has been used as a cure for sprains.

The Crab Apple is distantly related to the rose – its twigs have a thorn-like end – and it is still used as a rootstock for grafting garden varieties, which, if left to grow from seed, can mutate from their parents due to their complicated genetic strand, which contains around 57,000 genes – 20,000 more than the human genome.

The word 'apple' was widely used to describe any fruit up until the seventeenth century, and the forbidden fruit eaten by Adam and Eve could have been a fig, grape, pomegranate or quince – the Bible only mentions fruit from the 'tree of the knowledge of good and evil'. The belief that the apple was the forbidden fruit could be a misconception that has come about from the Latin *malus*, which, used as an adjective, means evil, but as a noun translates as apple. The tree could have been a mythological metaphor representing a higher knowledge.

Newton's Apple Tree
WOOLSTHORPE BY COLSTERWORTH, LINCOLNSHIRE 108
Apple, Flower of Kent (*Malus domestica*)

Sir Isaac Newton (1643– 1727) is recognised as one of the most influential English scientists. Educated at Cambridge, it was on returning to his childhood home at Woolsthorpe Manor that he made two discoveries that would change the scientific landscape forever. The first was his theory that white light was made up from a spectrum of refracted colours, and the second came about whilst he was observing an Apple tree in his garden:

*When formerly, the notion of gravitation came into his mind.
It was occasioned by the fall of an apple, as he sat in contemplative
mood. Why should that apple always descend perpendicularly to the
ground, thought he to himself. Why should it not go sideways or
upwards, but constantly to the Earth's centre.*

From *Memoirs of Sir Isaac Newton's Life*, William Stukeley, 1726

ABOVE: Newton contemplates a falling apple under the celebrated Apple tree.

OPPOSITE: Apple Tree at Woolsthorpe Manor, 2008.

Thus the theory of gravitation was born, but it would be another 20 years before Newton developed the theory that terrestrial gravity extends, decreasing over distance, to the Moon, enabling him to calculate its orbit and securing his name, along with England's most famous Apple tree, in the annals of history.

Around 200 years ago, the Apple tree in Newton's garden fell. It is unclear whether it regrew where it lay, or a descendant of the original tree took root. Either way, the tree that now stands at Woolsthorpe Manor marks the spot where the illustrious story occurred and continues to thrive to this day. Another descendant of the tree grows beneath the window of Newton's lodgings outside the main gate of Trinity College, Cambridge.

*She showed him an apple as green as grass,
She showed him a gay gold ring;
She showed him a cherry as red as blood,
And with that she'ticed him in!*

Traditional ballad

214

The Sweet Chestnut

Sweet Chestnut *(Castenea sativa)*

O CHESTNUT TREE, GREAT ROOTED BLOSSOMER,
ARE YOU THE LEAF, THE BLOSSOM OR THE BOLE?
O BODY SWAYED TO MUSIC, O BRIGHTENING GLANCE,
HOW CAN WE KNOW THE DANCER FROM THE DANCE.
FROM *AMONG SCHOOL CHILDREN*, WILLIAM BUTLER YEATS, C.1926

ABOVE: A large Sweet Chestnut with an 8-m (26-ft) girth at Cowdray Park in 2009.

OPPOSITE: A Sweet Chestnut tree and fallen trunk in the deer park at Studley Royal Water Garden, adjoining Fountains Abbey, North Yorkshire.

Probably introduced into Britain by the Romans almost 2,000 years ago, we could be forgiven for regarding the Sweet Chestnut tree as a native, so long has it featured in our cultural psyche. It is also known as the Spanish Chestnut, having originated in the Mediterranean.

Growing to a height of 30m (98.4ft) and capable of attaining a huge girth, the tree can live for centuries, and although it was beloved of the Romans for the sweet chestnut fruit it yields, it was not common in Britain until the sixteenth century when it was widely planted for its fruit, good timber and stately appearance. It was found to have properties not unlike Oak, responded well to coppicing and was used to make gates, posts and wine casks.

Long Chestnut avenues were planted on large estates, as the trees grew twice as fast as Oak and offered good shade for livestock and people alike – perfect for landscaping. The Chestnut was also found to have excellent properties for tanning and charcoal making.

The bark has characteristic deep ridges, often with a deep furrowed, swirling crosshatch pattern with age. The leaves are among the longest in Britain, with a distinctive saw-toothed edge, growing up to 25cm (10in); they can be infused as a remedy for respiratory complaints.

Today chestnuts are still popular roasted on open fires and used to make stuffings for meat and poultry, especially at Christmas. There are very few folk tales, proverbs and early songs associated with the tree in Britain, going some way to confirm that most of our folklore has its roots in the pagan age – before the coming of the Romans.

The Spanish Chestnut Avenue
CROFT CASTLE, HEREFORDSHIRE 109 🌿🍃

The Croft family built the castle that bears their name during the fifteenth century, and may have arrived from Normandy even before the Conquest. Ambrey Iron Age hill fort, which stands in the grounds of the park, confirms evidence of an earlier settlement, but it is the Crofts who firmly established themselves here, and they are still in residence today, almost 1,000 years later.

The castle held a strategic position in the Welsh Marches: John Croft married one of Owain Glendywr's daughters in the fifteenth century. However, holding on to the estate did not come without its problems. Around 1750, the family was forced to sell the manor due to financial difficulties, but they managed to return in 1923 and cement their territorial pedigree.

Today the castle sits in 1,500 acres of woodland, farmland and parkland, and it has fine avenues of veteran Oak, Beech and more recently planted Lime trees. But perhaps the most interesting of these is the Spanish Chestnut Avenue, which runs for a kilometre (0.62 miles) to the west of the castle. Legend suggests that the trees were planted using chestnuts retrieved from the wrecks of the Spanish Armada in 1592. Arranged in ranks to represent the warship's battle lines, some of the trees are over 400 years old with boles measuring between 8 and 9m (26 and 29.5ft) in girth.

Myths persist of survivors from the Armada settling in various locations around the English, Scottish and Irish coasts as they fled north in defeat from the English Channel. Of the 130 ships that set sail from Spain, only around half would return; the others were wrecked in storms. As many as 2,000 sailors and soldiers drowned – over 1,000 bodies are said to have been washed up on a single beach. Many survivors were rounded up and killed whereas some rich or eminent ones were held for ransom and eventually returned home, but the Armada's refugees do not seem to have left such a lasting impact as the Chestnut Avenue at Croft.

There is time to finish the game and beat the Spaniards too.

Sir Francis Drake on being informed of the arrival of the Spanish Armada in 1588, whilst playing bowls on Plymouth Hoe.

ABOVE: *The Spanish Armada, 1588* by Philip James de Loutherbourg (1740–1812).

ABOVE: The Church and east front of Croft Castle.

OPPOSITE: The Spanish Chestnut Avenue at Croft Castle.

The Tortworth Chestnut

TORTWORTH, GLOUCESTERSHIRE 110

As you approach the Tortworth Chestnut in the churchyard of St Leonards, you wonder where in this small wood is the tree? But the wood is the tree – branches over centuries have drooped to the ground and re-rooted, growing into new stems still joined to their parent, and saplings have sprung from the copious fruits that the tree still produces. Although it is a mess, nevertheless it remains a very beautiful and awe-inspiring site.

The tree was known as the 'Great Chestnut of Tortworth' in King Stephen's reign (1135–1154), and was marked as a boundary tree to the manor of Tortworth a century later when King John held the throne. In 1766, the *Gentlemen's Magazine* declared the trunk to be 50ft (15.24m) in circumference, and by 1830, Jacob George Strutt had it at 52ft (15.85m). It now stands with a girth of 11m (36ft) but it has lost several branches over the centuries.

A plaque near the tree dated 1 January 1800 supposes it to be 600 years old on that date, which would make it 800 years old today. That being the case, the tree would have to have been planted sometime around 1200, but it was well known as a great tree about 100 years previous to that in Stephen's time. It stands to reason therefore that the tree must be in excess of 1,000 years old, making it the largest and most aged Chestnut in the country, and I see no reason to doubt it.

May man still guard
thy venerable form,
from the rude blasts,
and tempestuous storm.
Still mayest thou flourish
through succeeding time,
and last, long last,
the wonder of the clime.

Inscription on plaque erected in 1800

ABOVE: The Tortworth Chestnut, *c.* 1920.
OPPOSITE: The Tortworth Chestnut in 2008.

Queen Elizabeth's Tree

GREENWICH PARK, GREATER LONDON III

Greenwich Park offers spectacular views towards the River Thames and its eastern approach from the sea, making it a strategic vantage point, which has been exploited for two millennia. The Romans had a settlement there from AD49, and the Saxons from 550. Later on, the Danes improved on its defences, and after the Norman invasion of 1066 it became a manor, later being enclosed in 1433 to form London's first Royal park.

Henry VIII was born at the Palace built there by his father Henry VII, as were his two daughters Mary and Elizabeth, and it is Elizabeth who concerns us here. A large Chestnut tree, which was planted in the twelfth century, played host to the young princess – she is said to have played there as a child and picnicked inside the hollow trunk. Her father is even rumoured to have danced round the tree with Anne Boleyn. A door and window facing the adjacent hill were later installed with a tiled floor and bench, which could seat 15 people. In the seventeenth century, it was used as a lock-up to detain park offenders.

The last living shoots on the tree were noted in 1878. This may explain why it became known as Elizabeth's Oak – without foliage as a guide, tree identification can be difficult – but it was clearly marked on the first edition Ordnance Survey map as the 'Old Chestnut Tree' in1894. On publication of the second edition, however, it was marked as Queen Elizabeth's Oak. Around this time, it was measured at 6m (19.6ft) in girth.

The dead tree defied the great storm of 1987, but eventually collapsed on 2 July 1991. Heavy rains softened the soil and washed the mass of ivy from its trunk – the structure that had supported the decaying hulk – as clearly visible on the archive photograph. Ivy rarely suffocates its host, and in this case it acted as a crutch. On examination, experts confirmed that it was indeed a Chestnut tree. On 4 July 1992, HRH Prince Philip planted an Oak nearby in memory of the venerable old Chestnut.

OPPOSITE: Queen Elizabeth's Tree in 2010.

The old oak referred to, beneath which Royalty have frequently congregated, must, in its heyday, have been a tree of giant proportions, the hollowed trunk in which Queen Elizabeth oft partook of refreshments, and where offenders against the Park rules have been confined, being fully twenty feet in girth, while the internal cavity is six feet in diameter.

Greenwich Park: Its History & Associations, A D Webster, 1902

ABOVE: Queen Elizabeth's Tree in 1920.

223

The Dinton Chestnut

DINTON PARK, WILTSHIRE II2 🌿🍃

Dinton Park sits in the Nadder Valley in the shadow of Wick Ball Camp, an Iron Age hill fort, and boasts a large number of veteran trees covering a myriad of species in some 200 acres of parkland.

Dinton belonged to Shaftesbury Abbey at the time of the Domesday Survey, and remained so until the dissolution when the manor eventually passed into the hands of Sir William Herbert, later Earl of Pembroke, in 1547. William Wyndham purchased the estate in 1689 and built a house there, and in the garden sits a huge Spanish Chestnut tree, hidden amongst undergrowth until closer inspection. It was most likely planted around the time of Wyndham's purchase but could well have been there before. I watched Ted Green and Jill Butler from the Woodland Trust measure it at a collossal 10m (32.8ft) in girth. On a previous visit to the tree a large adder had calmly slid away from the dappled sunlight below the branches where it had been warming itself.

The house was rebuilt completely in 1816 and remained in the possession of the Wyndham family, handed down from father to son, until 1916 when it was sold to Bertram Erasmus Phillips, who renamed it Phillips House. In 1943, he gave the house and park to the National Trust, which continues to manage it today.

A sailor's wife had chestnuts in her lap,
And mounched and mounched
* and mounched.*
'Give me,' quoth I.
'Aroint thee, witch!'
* the rump-fed ronyon cries.*

From Macbeth, William Shakespeare

OPPOSITE: The great Dinton Chestnut, 2008.
BELOW: Phillips House in 2009.

CHAPTER NINE

The Sycamore

Sycamore (*Acer pseudoplatanus*)

THE SYCAMORE, CAPRICIOUS IN ATTIRE,
NOW GREEN, NOW TAWNY, AND ERE AUTUMN YET
HAS CHANGED THE WOODS, IN SCARLET HONOURS BRIGHT.
WILLIAM COWPER (1731–1800)

ABOVE: Winged Sycamore seed.
OPPOSITE: The Great Sycamore at Birnam, Perthshire, is 300 years old with a girth of 8m (26.2ft).

The Sycamore, also known as the Great Maple or, in some parts of Scotland, the Plane Tree, grows to 38m (124.6ft) in height with straight branches, twisting twigs and flaking plated bark. The large five-lobed leaves are rarely seen without the now familiar blotchy black spots, which are caused by the tar spot fungus. Native to central Europe, the Sycamore has been grown in Britain for at least 500 years and may have been introduced by the Romans, but it has become fully naturalised, making it the bane of many a gardener as its seedlings swamp out other plants. Far from being a weed, the Sycamore can grow into a magnificent and large tree.

It is nowhere found, wild or natural, in our land, that I can learn; but only planted in orchards or walkes for the shadowes sake.

From *Theatrum Botanicum*, John Parkinson, 1640

A hardy species, the tree fares well in Scotland and the north, and it provides a good white timber. Scottish children are said in times past to have cut the trunk to drink the sweet sugary sap that flows from the wound. By fermentation, elder Scots would brew it into wine. In the west of their country, an old name for the tree was 'Dool', or sorrow tree, so named as the tree of choice for the gibbet up until the 1750s.

ABOVE: A 5-m (16.4-ft) girthed Sycamore at Frome, Somerset.

The Tewin Grave

TEWIN, HERTFORDSHIRE 113 🌿

The ancient village of Tewin probably takes its name from the Norse god of war Tew – from whence the origin of Tuesday on our weekly calendar comes – but there is evidence to suggest that the area was populated long before the arrival of the Saxons.

St Peter's Church, the oldest surviving building in the village, was built around 604 on the site of an ancient Temple of Tew. Rebuilt in 1086 with the arrival of the Normans, it slowly developed into the building seen today. However, by far the most visited relic on the site is the tomb of one Lady Anne Grimstone, the widow of Sir Samuel Grimstone, who died at Tewin House on 22 November 1713, aged 60. On her deathbed, she is reputed to have said:

> *If indeed there is life hereafter,*
> *trees will render my tomb asunder.*

She was buried in a marble tomb at the east end of the churchyard, which, after some time, showed signs of a crack, through which a tree started to grow. Multi-stemmed Ash and Sycamore trees forced their way through, eventually engulfing the tomb and almost breaking it apart.

In 1870, iron railings were erected to protect the site from souvenir hunters, but these, in turn, were absorbed by the trees, traces of which can be seen in the recent photograph (right). Newer railings were installed some safe distance from the tomb. The Ash is long gone, leaving only the four-stemmed Sycamore alive.

Whether Lady Anne Grimstone was an atheist or not is open to debate, as the records affirm that she regularly attended the church services at Tewin, but her story certainly offers food for thought to the congregation, and it ensures that sightseers and tourists continue to visit her grave to this day.

OPPOSITE: The Tewin Grave in 1915.
BELOW: The Tewin Grave in 2010.

The Martyrs' Tree
TOLPUDDLE, DORSET 114 🌿🍃

In 1834, six agricultural labourers from Tolpuddle in Dorset were sentenced to serve seven years' transportation – hard labour in Australia from which few ever returned – for standing up for their rights and effectively starting the trade union movement in Britain.

They had recently fallen victim to three vicious pay cuts, lowering their wages from nine to six shillings a week, and could no longer afford to support their families. George Loveless, his brother James, James Hammett, James Brine, Thomas Standfield and his son John, met beneath a large Sycamore tree on the village green to discuss what they could do to address their situation. The men formed a trade union – which worried the local squire James Frampton greatly – but this in itself was not illegal, so they were eventually charged with having taken an illegal secret oath.

When the men left for Australia, their families had to fend for themselves and were supported only by donations from a union campaign. However, there was a huge public outcry at the unjust treatment of the Tolpuddle Martyrs, which culminated in a march through London by 100,000 people. Their plea for freedom could not be ignored, and the six men were eventually granted full pardons on 14 March 1836, and returned home to Tolpuddle.

To commemorate the centenary of the Martyrs in 1934, Sir Ernest Debenham gave the village green to the National Trust, in whose care it remains. In honour of the Martyrs, the Sycamore still stands strong, with a girth of 5.9m (19.35ft), and was calculated by Ray Hawes, Head of Forestry at the National Trust, to be around 330 years old. This means that the tree was already of substantial size when the Martyrs met beneath its branches in 1834.

Thousands of visitors pay their respects to the Martyrs' Tree every year. It has become a place of pilgrimage for trade unionists, for whom a festival is held at Tolpuddle every July.

God is our guide no sword we draw,
We kindle not wars battle fires,
By reason, union, justice, law,
We claim the birthright of our sires.
We raise the watchword Liberty,
We will, we will, we will be free.

George Loveless (1797–1874)

ABOVE: Bole of the Martyrs' Tree and monument, 2009.

OPPOSITE: The Martyrs' Tree in 2009.

CHAPTER TEN

The London Plane

London Plane *(Platinus x hispanica)*

ABOVE: The round fruits of the Plane tree.
OPPOSITE: London Plane trees in Soho Square, 2009.

The London Plane is a cross between the Oriental and American Plane trees, but opinion is still divided as to whether the first hybrid was grown in Spain or southern France around 1650, or in London itself. The seventeenth-century botanist John Tradescant certainly had both varieties growing in his garden in 1636 and he was responsible for introducing the American variant to British climes, so many regard him as the originator. Either way, the tree is now so familiar in London that it accounts for around half of the city's total tree population.

Towering to a height of 44m (144.3ft), the London Plane has long, spreading, irregular branches and five-lobed leaves, which are not dissimilar to those of the Sycamore, only larger and more pointed. The smooth, grey bark peels off annually in large platelets – making it perfectly suited to city life – helping the tree to protect itself from the effects of pollution, along with its shiny, tough leaves, which are easily washed in the rain. One wartime story tells how army colonels offered a reward for information regarding what they thought was deliberate bark-stripping by delinquents. The distinctive round catkins hang throughout the winter, like spiky Christmas baubles.

The earliest surviving specimens of the tree still thrive for more than 320 years after planting, displaying huge boles and magnificent crowns. Aptly named the 'Cockney Tree' by Marcus Woodward in his *New Book of Trees*, *c.*1920, the London Plane is prolific in most British cities, and is certainly a contender to become one of the island's most common future ancients in a changing British treescape.

Berkeley Square Planes

BERKELEY SQUARE, LONDON 115

The London Planes in Berkeley Square are the oldest living trees in central London, and they were planted in 1789 by Edward Bouverie, resident at number 13 and the son of Jacob des Bouverie, 1st Viscount of Folkestone. At over 220 years old, the trees are in great shape, the largest having grown to a height of 30m (98.4ft) with a girth of 6m (19.6ft). It has been named the 'Berkeley Plane' and was listed as one of the top 20 London trees by the charity Trees for London. In 2008, the Berkeley Plane was valued at £750,000, making it London's most valuable tree. London Tree Officers took the initiative of valuing London's trees in an effort to stop any more being cut down at the request of insurance companies, which were eager to blame them for housing subsidence. All too often, trees were lost before a proper assessment could be made.

Berkeley Square was first enclosed in 1747, forming a water meadow on the north bank of the then still open Tyburn stream. Like most of London's natural waterways, the Tyburn now runs unnoticed beneath the city streets. The square was named after John Berkeley who took possession of the land adjacent to Berkeley House, and developed it over a period of 30 years to the layout recognised today.

In 1940, Manning Sherwin and Eric Maschwitz published a song entitled *A Nightingale Sang in Berkeley Square*. It was performed by a host of major artists, including Vera Lynn, Frank Sinatra and, later, Rod Stewart, and was destined to become a standard. In 1941, the iron railings enclosing the park were removed to help with the war effort, and American troops were stationed there.

Today, the square is a green oasis for Londoners, an antithesis to frenetic city life, and the fact that nightingales probably never sang in Berkeley Square does nothing to quieten the robins that do sing there.

I may be right, I may be wrong,
But I'm perfectly willing to swear
That when you turn'd and smiled at me
A Nightingale Sang In Berkeley Square.

From *A Nightingale Sang in Berkeley Square*, Manning Sherwin and Eric Maschwitz, 1940

OPPOSITE: The Berkeley Square Plane in 2010.
BELOW: Berkeley Square, c. 1925.

The Abbey Green Plane
BATH, AVON 116

Green is the plane-tree in the square,
The other trees are brown;
They droop and pine for country air;
The plane-tree loves the town.

From *A London Plane-Tree*, Amy Levy, 1889

Bath has a rich and ancient history. According to legend, it was founded in 860BC by Prince Bladud, the father of King Lear, who was cured of leprosy whilst bathing in the healing waters of Bath springs. The Romans took full advantage of the hot springs and built their famous baths at the site some 900 years later – a pastime still enjoyed by residents and visitors alike at the new Bath Spa, which was completely rebuilt and opened in 2006.

Bath can consider itself lucky to have been largely redeveloped in the eighteenth century, when it became a fashionable spa resort for the wealthy. Its legacy is an exemplary heritage of Georgian architecture. Planning laws still stipulate the use of local Bath stone, lending the city a uniform, but warm, honey colour.

The city's most magnificent tree must be the Plane in Abbey Square just south of the medieval Abbey. It was planted *c.*1790, around the same time as the Berkeley Square Planes, suggesting that the genus had by then become fashionable.

The tree dominates the square with a huge crown and girth of over 6m (19.6ft). It was photographed in the early 1900s with an iron cage around its bole, which it had practically absorbed by the 1930s. Today it is left unbound, proving, after more than two centuries, that it can look after itself.

OPPOSITE: The Abbey Green Plane, *c.*1920.

The name of Nelson in Bath is on everyone's lips.

Nelson's father writing to his son

BELOW: The Abbey Green Plane in 2010.

The Great Plane

MOTTISFONT ABBEY, HAMPSHIRE 117

The Great Plane at Mottisfont sits in the abbey gardens between the house and the west bank of a tributary of the River Test. It is the largest of its species in the country, with branches that cover an area of 1,500 square metres (16,146 square feet), and a bole that measures 11.81m (38.74ft) in circumference.

It was planted in 1740 by Sir Richard Mill as he extended the house and gardens, making it contemporary with the current Georgian-styled house. Other Planes planted by Mill at around the same time have not reached such massive proportions, and the dual stem of the tree has led experts to speculate that the Great Plane is in fact two trees that have melded together over many years. Another explanation is that the tree was pollarded at a young age, its rapid growth promoted by a plentiful supply of water drawn from the ever-flowing Test.

The name Mottisfont probably derives from the Saxon 'moot', meaning to meet, reflecting stories of Saxon meetings, and the old English or Latin 'font', meaning fountain or spring, in honour of the spring that flows into the head of the stream.

A priory was established there in 1201 by William Briwere, an adviser to Richard the Lionheart, King John and Henry III and also one of the signatories of Magna Carta. The small foundation played host to a valuable relic – the forefinger of St John the Baptist – which had baptised Jesus. It was guarded by the eleven or so canons, and Mottisfont became a place of pilgrimage.

It is not clear what happened to the famous finger but it was probably lost in the dissolution of the monasteries, for in 1536, the priory and lands were exchanged for the villages of Chelsea and Paddington, and were conveyed to William Lord Sandys who converted the priory into a Tudor house.

In 1934, Gilbert Russell, a descendant of William Briwere, bought the estate, which after his death was given to the National Trust by his wife in 1957. The grounds are still rich with ancient specimens of Oak, Chestnut, Beech, and Hornbeam, including the Oakley Oak – a 10.74-m (35.23-ft) girthed tree beside the neighbouring Oakley stream – which probably predates the priory.

I baptize with water: but there standeth one among you, whom ye know not; He it is, who coming after me is preferred before me, whose shoe's latchet I am not worthy to unloose.

St John 1:26

ABOVE: The Great Plane in 2005.

OPPOSITE: The Great Plane (in background to the left) beside Mottisfont Abbey in 2008.

CHAPTER ELEVEN

The Walnut

Common Walnut (*Juglans regia*)

ABOVE: Walnut Flower.

OPPOSITE: The Black Walnut tree at Antony House, Cornwall.

The first reference to the Walnut in British literature appears in the 1567 edition of *Encyclopaedia Britannica*, but it was probably introduced much earlier by the Romans via Greece, originating from Persia.

The Walnut grows to 30m (98.4ft) in height, and occasionally yields magnificent ancient trees with sprawling, twisting oak-like branches. The leaves are similar to those of the Ash but larger, appearing in pairs of seven to nine leaflets.

The Common, or English, Walnut is the most frequently found variety in Britain, but the name 'English' is itself misleading. It became associated with the trees in medieval times due to English merchant sailors who transported them on their travels around the world. The next most widespread variety is the American Walnut, or Black Walnut (*Juglans nigra*), which can grow to even larger proportions than its English counterpart.

Prized for its fruit, providing a favourite edible nut (which grows best only in a good summer), the Walnut also produces our most valuable timber. The trees are dug out, never felled, as the best wood comes from the base of the trunk and has been used extensively in a wide range of products from Regency furniture to Jaguar dashboards.

The Latin name *juglans* translates as 'Jupiter's acorn' while *regia* means 'royal', so the fruit can rightly be described as Royal Jupiter's acorn – food of the gods. However, the tree has a sinister side to its nature, secreting a poison called juglone from its roots, and this is capable of killing most tree species that grow nearby.

The Bexhill Walnut

BEXHILL, SUSSEX 118

The modern seaside town of Bexhill did not develop until the late nineteenth century, but the old town further inland has its first mention in 771 when King Offa claimed to have defeated the men of Hastings. He granted a charter there the following year.

The Bexhill Walnut stood in the old town beside Manor Gardens, a thirteenth-century manor house at the junction of the High Street and Upper Sea Road. The land between here and the sea was an unpopulated marshland in the eighteenth century, and Sea Road provided access to the coast for local fishermen, but it was also a route notorious for smugglers who would use it to traffic their booty inland. Stories abound of the smugglers' violence and ruthlessness in protecting their illicit trade, in defiance of authority and often ending in deaths on both sides. They would no doubt have known the Walnut tree and passed it many times on their forays to and from the coast.

At the time of the photograph, dated 1895, the Walnut was in good health, with a large spreading crown protected by a brick wall and iron railings, but less than a decade later, the tree had been severely pollarded, and it is difficult to see why. Perhaps it was deemed unsafe, which would provide a good excuse for removing it and accessing some valuable timber. Shortly afterwards the tree was completely removed by the local council. It survives in a small way as a gavel that was turned from the tree and is still used by Bexhill Council to keep order at council meetings.

A tea room named the Walnut Tree trades round the corner in the High Street in honour of this great tree. Apart from the sylvan loss, the scene remains much the same today as it was a century ago.

BELOW: The Bexhill Walnut in 1895.

ABOVE: The Bexhill Walnut in 1903.

The Bossington Walnut

The National Trust has cared for the Holnicote Estate since 1944. Covering an area of over 12,000 acres, close to the coast in the heart of Exmoor, the estate includes the picturesque villages of Bossington and Selworthy, and the ancient Horner Wood, home to hundreds of impressive 700-year-old Oaks.

The villages are rich in Walnut trees. They were planted on the Holnicote Estate to provide wood for gunstocks, which, being light and strong and not vulnerable to splitting or warping, the timber – known as heartwood – was ideally suited.

At Bossington, beside the road at Walnut Tree Cottage, stood a tree that was reputed to be England's largest Walnut and which survived until January 1952 when it was cut down. The cottage still stands, its large chimney breast concealing the bread oven at its base, a feature common with most of the cottages in the area.

Up until 1815, when the village opened its first church, which was built entirely from money raised by local fundraising, services were often held inside the cottage, in the shadow of the great Walnut.

ABOVE: The Bossington Walnut, c. 1940.

LEFT: An ancient coppiced Oak in Horner Wood, c. 2005.

243

The Selworthy Walnut

SELWORTHY, SOMERSET 120

Two miles from Bossington lies the scenic village of Selworthy, with its picture-postcard thatched cottages, lime-washed with a creamy yellow ochre tint. At first glance they appear ancient, but the dwellings were not built until 1828 when Sir Thomas Dyke Acland, who acquired the village by marriage in 1802, had them constructed for the benefit of the old and infirm.

The Selworthy Walnut grew in the garden at Bow Cottage, nestled on a hillside in the shadow of the Iron Age hill fort of Bury Castle. The hill is Selworthy Beacon, one of the highest points on Exmoor, which offers spectacular views towards Porlock bay.

The cottage survives the tree, which is now lost, but judging from this photograph it rivalled the Walnut at Bossington if not in girth then certainly by the spread of its sprawling and twisted limbs.

Sir Richard Acland, heir to the estate passed down through his family for almost 150 years, gave it to the National Trust in 1944.

Then I heard that fearful sound...the sharp yet solemn sound of trees burst open by the frost-blow. Our great walnut lost three branches, and has been dying ever since; though growing meanwhile, as the soul does.

From *Lorna Doone – A Romance of Exmoor*, R D Blackmore, 1869

OPPOSITE: The Selworthy Walnut, c.1940.
BELOW: Bow Cottage at Selworthy, c.2005.

245

CHAPTER TWELVE

The Hawthorn

Hawthorn (*Crataegus monogyna* var. *biflora*)

AND THE MILKMAID SINGETH BLITHE,
AND THE MOWER WHETS HIS SCYTHE,
AND EVERY SHEPHERD TELLS HIS TALE
UNDER THE HAWTHORN IN THE DALE.
FROM *L'ALLEGRO*, JOHN MILTON, 1631

ABOVE: Haw growing on the Glastonbury Thorn at St John's Church, Glastonbury, 2008.

OPPOSITE: Windblown Hawthorn tree at Crowlink, part of the Seven Sisters Cliffs, East Sussex.

The Hawthorn is a slow-growing tree, living typically up to 200 years, but sometimes much longer – a tree in the village of Hethel, Norfolk, is thought to be 700 years old. Reaching 15m (49.2ft) in height, the thorny tree has lobed leaves, producing white flowers in spring and deep red haws in autumn.

The variety *biflora* is included here amongst invaders and settlers, but the common variant is native and synonymous with British traditions. In pagan times, faeries were thought to reside around solitary hawthorns, which marked entrances to the Celtic Underworld.

The spring flowering of the Hawthorn led to it being named 'The May Tree'. A Suffolk tradition entitled any servant who could deliver a blossoming branch to their farmhouse on the first day of May to a dish of cream for breakfast, but the change to the Gregorian calendar in 1752 meant the flowering occurred nearer the middle of the month.

Blossoms were often set outside houses, but to bring them inside was taboo, believed to be followed by a death. Indeed, the scent of the blossom was held to be the smell of death. It was later discovered to contain trimethylamine – a chemical found in decaying tissue.

Richard III, last of the Plantagenet kings, was killed at the Battle of Bosworth in 1485. His crown was said to have been hidden in a Hawthorn bush, but was later found by Lord Stanley and taken to the victor Henry who claimed the throne. A crown on a flowering Hawthorn was adopted as an emblem by the Tudors, and spawned the proverb: 'Cling to the crown though it hang from a bush'.

The Holy Thorn

GLASTONBURY, SOMERSET 121 🍃

After the crucifixion, legend says that Joseph of Arimathea, Jesus's great uncle, sailed to Britain to spread the word of the gospel. He landed at Avalon (Glastonbury – a lake island at the time) and thrust his hawthorn staff into the ground where it immediately took root as a Hawthorn tree. This was at Wearyall Hill, so named after the long and arduous journey from Palestine, as Joseph and his company were 'weary all'.

The tree is unique amongst Hawthorns for producing white flowers twice a year, in spring and in winter, marking the birth and resurrection of Jesus. Its unorthodox planting could allude to an early form of grafting with a cutting – the only way the tree will grow and flower twice. But the original Hawthorn could have been a species introduced by Crusaders on their return from Palestine.

The thorn was cut down and burned as a superstitious relic by a Puritan soldier in 1653, during the Civil War, but retribution was swift, when the thorns blinded one of his eyes in the process.

A cutting from the original tree was secretly replanted at Wearyall Hill where it remains to this day, and also at nearby Glastonbury Abbey and St John's Church. James Montague, Bishop of Bath and Wells, sent a branch to Queen Anne in the seventeenth century, a tradition that is upheld to the present day. Currently the pupils from St John's School send a sprig to Queen Elizabeth from the churchyard, which can be seen on her desk when she makes her Christmas speech to the nation.

On 8 December 2010, the day a sprig was cut for the Queen, somebody climbed Wearyall Hill in the dead of night and cut the head from the tree, severing all the branches. Opinions were divided as to whether it was outright vandalism or essential pollarding, but the roots were undamaged, and in 2011, new shoots emerged from the base of the trunk. Two thousand years on from its 'miracle' birth, like Christ himself, the thorn appears to have risen again.

To Glastonbury, where the winter thorn Blossoms at Christmas, mindful of Our Lord.

From *The Holy Grail*, **Alfred, Lord Tennyson (1809–1892)**

248

A vast concourse of people attended the noted thorn on Christmas-day, new style; but, to their great disappointment, there was no appearance of its blowing, which made them watch it narrowly the 5th of January, the Christmas-day, old style, when it blowed as usual.

From *The Gentleman's Magazine*, **January 1753**

ABOVE: The Glastonbury Thorn (now gone) at the ruins of Glastonbury Abbey, *c.* 1925.

ABOVE: The Glastonbury Thorn cut down, 2010.
OPPOSITE: The Glastonbury Thorn, Wearyall Hill, in 2008.

APPENDICES

Bibliography and Further Reading

AA Illustrated Guide to Britain, Collins Publishers (1976)

Bainbridge, John, *New Forest Photographic Memories*, the Francis Frith Collection (2001)

Collins Gem Trees, HarperCollins Publishers (1980)

Cotterell, Arthur, *Norse Mythology*, Sebastian Kelly (1998)

Evelyn, John, *Sylva, Vol. 1* or *A Discourse of Forest Trees* (1670)

Johnson, Hugh, *The International Book of Trees*, Mitchell Beazley Publishers Ltd (1973)

Johnson, Owen, and More, David, *Collins Tree Guide*, HarperCollins Publishers (2006)

Lacey, Stephen, *Gardens of the National Trust*, National Trust Books Ltd (2005)

Lowe, John, *The Yew Trees of Britain and Ireland*, Macmillan and Co. (1897)

Marshall, H E, *Our Island Story*, T C & E C Jack (*c.*1910)

Miles, Archie, *The Trees That Made Britain*, BBC Books (2006)

Packenham, Thomas, *Meetings with Remarkable Trees*, Weidenfeld & Nicolson (1996)

Packenham, Thomas, *Remarkable Trees of the World*, Weidenfeld & Nicolson (2002)

Pocket Trees, Dorling Kindersley Ltd (1995)

Robson, Forster, *British Trees and How to Name Them*, Holden and Harlington (*c.*1915)

Spence, Lewis, *The Mysteries of Britain – Secret Rites & Traditions of Ancient Britain*, Senate (1994)

Strutt, Jacob George, *Sylva Britannica or Portraits of Forest Trees* (1826)

The Martyrs of Tolpuddle, the TUC (1934)

The National Trust Guide, Jonathan Cape Ltd (1976)

Thompson, Andy, *Native British Trees*, Wooden Hill Books (2005)

White, Gilbert, *The Natural History of Selborne* (1788)

Wilkes, J H, *Trees of The British Isles in History & Legend*, Frederick Muller Ltd (1972)

Woodward, Marcus, *The New Book of Trees*, A M Philpot (*c.*1920)

Useful websites

In addition to the books listed above, I trawled a myriad of websites – too many to mention – and the following proved invaluable:

www.nationaltrust.org.uk
www.ancient-tree-hunt.org.uk
www.ancient-yew.org
http://frontpage.woodland-trust.org.uk/ancient-tree-forum/
http://en.wikipedia.org/wiki/Main_Page
www.hainaultforest.co.uk
www.savernakeestate.co.uk

National Trust Ancient Trees and Woodlands

The conservation of trees and woodlands has been an important part of the National Trust's work for over 100 years since its first wood, Brandelhow, in Borrowdale, Cumbria, was bought in 1902. Now the National Trust manages hundreds of woods extending over at least 25,000ha (61,776 acres) in England, Wales and Northern Ireland, including commercial conifer plantations as well as some of the oldest woodlands in these islands.

In all woodlands the aim is to maximise their value to people and wildlife, now and for the future, using a combination of modern and traditional woodland management techniques. Ancient trees provide a valuable habitat, hosting rare fungi, lichens and deadwood invertebrates, many of which are totally dependent on ancient trees for their survival.

A huge survey is currently in progress (with funding from Cadbury) whereby the National Trust will record the condition of each specimen to ensure that there are enough replacement ancient trees for the future. With more than 25,000 hectares of woodland, 200,000 hectares of farmland and 135 landscape and deer-parks, more than 40,000 ancient trees are expected to be included in the survey during the next three years, although a large number remain unsurveyed and unrecorded to date.

Further information on trees and their locations can be found at **www.nationaltrust.org.uk**

Top National Trust sites to see ancient trees

Ashridge, Berkhamsted, Hertfordshire
Attingham Park, Shropshire
Beddgelert, Snowdonia (Gelert's Grave)
Borrowdale, Seathwaite, Cumbria
(The Borrowdale Yews)
Calke Abbey, Derbyshire (The Old Man of Calke)
Chirk Castle, North East Wales
Clumber Park, Worksop, Nottinghamshire
(Clumber Park Lime Avenue)
Croft Castle, Herefordshire (The Spanish Chestnuts)
Crom Estate, Northern Ireland
Dinefwr, South Wales
Dunham Massey, Greater Manchester
Florence Court, Co. Fermanagh
(The Original Irish Yew)
Fountains Abbey & Studley Royal, Ripon, Yorkshire
(Studley Royal Wild Cherry, Fountains Abbey Yews)
Hatfield Forest, Takeley, Essex
Holnicote Estate, Somerset (Horner Wood)
Killerton, Devon
Kingston Lacy, Dorset (The Beech Avenue)
Lanhydrock, Cornwall
Mottisfont Abbey, Hampshire (The Great Plane)
Petworth, West Sussex
Philipps House & Dinton Park, Wiltshire
(Dinton Park Chestnut)
Runnymede, Old Windsor, Surrey
(The Ankerwyke Yew)
Scotney Castle, Kent
Stourhead, Wiltshire
Tolpuddle, Dorset (The Martyr's Tree)
Wallington, Northumberland
Woolsthorpe Manor, Woolsthorpe, Lincolnshire
(Newton's Apple Tree)

Index

Picture Credits

ROLL OF HONOUR

A debt of gratitude to the following who showed faith over the course of the three years it took to develop this book: My family; Charlotte and Jake for their unlimited patience and support, my companion and model on numerous field trips Harry Hight. My parents David and Pauline and sister Louise. Bill Cathcart at Windsor Great Park, Ray Hawes at National Trust, Cathy Gosling at Anova, Duncan Baird, Anne-Marie Doulton, Julia Skinner, Emma Worth and David Partner.

Thanks to Michael Marra for permission to quote his song; 'Niel Gow's Apprentice' published by B.A.T Music.

Photo acknowledgements

I would like to thank the following for submitting photographs free of charge at some considerable effort to themselves: Adrian Sanders, Clive Brewin, David Partner, Heather Crisp, Ian Elphick, Jake Hight, Keith Harris, Laton Frewen, Louise Woodall and Iris Avery, Peter Horne, Rod Jewell, Skipton Castle, Strathleven Artisans, Sue Molloy and Alison Reilly, Terry Sackett.

PICTURE CREDITS

All photographs and engravings © Julian Hight except:
p24 left © Archie Miles Photography
p24 © Strathleven Artizans
p25 © Stirling Smith Art Gallery & Museum, RCAHMS Enterprises
p26 bottom © Lancashire County Council
p27 bottom © Peter Horne
p31 top © Louise Woodall
pp38–39, 208–209 © Brian Muelaner
p40 right, 41 © Alison Reilly
p43 left © English Heritage Photo Library/ Boris Baggs
p51 left © Ian Elphick
p58 left © Jake Hight
p67 left © V&A Images
p83 right by kind permission of Viscount De L'Isle
p92 left © Laton Frewen
p106 © Barrie Pictures

p112 © David Partner
pp50 bottom, 85, 105 right, 129 © The Francis Frith Colllection
p159 © Richard Comotto
p178 By kind permission of Skipton Castle, Yorkshire
p180 left © Clive Brewin
p180 right, 181 © Rod Jewell
p183 © Hulton Archive/Fox Photos/Getty Images
p200, 201 © Heather Crisp
p204, 230, 231, 239 © Adrian Sanders
p214 © Mary Evans Picture Library
p236 © Bath in Time

© The National Trust Photo Library
NTPL/ Britainonview/ Rod Edwards: p152; NTPL/Andrew Butler: p2, 216, 240; NTPL/ David Caldwell: p10; NTPL/Joe Cornish: p11; NTPL/ Simon Fraser: p174; NTPL/Ross

Hoddinot: p206, 207;NTPL/David Levenson: p7; NTPL/ Rosie Mayer: p238; NTPL/John Miller: p244; NTPL/ Robert Morris: p219, 224; NTPL/ Tessa Musgrave: p215; NTPL/Stephen Robson: p9,153; NTPL/ Mark Sunderland: p157; NTPL/ Rupert Truman: p218; NTPL/ Paul Wakefield: p152 right, 243, 250;NTPL/J. Whitaker: p68–69.

My thanks to the following for granting permission to take photographs on private land:
The Crown Estate for Windsor Great Park, City of London Corporation for Burnham Beeches and The Guildhall, London, The Royal Parks for Greenwich Park, Kensington Gardens, Richmond Park, the trustees of Savernake Forest and the many church yards and parks that I visited around Britain.